THE *illustrated* GLASGOW GLOSSARY

Awra Words Awragirra

illustrated by Maria Holland

Albert Mackie

THE
BLACKSTAFF
PRESS

The Blackstaff Press Limited
3 Galway Park, Dundonald, Belfast BT16 0AN

First published in 1984
by The Blackstaff Press

Phototypeset in 10 on 12 point Sabon
by The Blackstaff Press
Printed in Northern Ireland
by W & G Baird Ltd

British Library Cataloguing in Publication Data

Mackie, Albert
The illustrated Glasgow glossary
1. English language – Dialects – Scotland – Glasgow (Strathclyde)
I. Title
427'.9414'43   PE2274.G57

ISBN 0 85640 304 0

Introduction

Glescaranto, the language of Scotland's Second-to-None City, is neither Gaelic nor Lallans, but a highly flexible mixture of Scots-English and Lanarkshire Scots, with Highland and Irish influences. Glasgow is a Keltic town (to spell it 'Celtic' would be to cause misunderstanding among Rangers supporters) and the local speech is soft and melodic on a descending scale. It is lavish with vowels and the letter *r*, with its kettledrum roll, but it is cavalier in its treatment of consonants, especially *d*, *t* and *th*, which tend to be strangled at birth. 'Motherwell,' for instance, becomes 'Murrawell' and 'altogether' becomes 'awragirra.'

The *Glossary* is a brave attempt at spelling the unspellable, but it is written in the hope that people from abroad, including Sassenachs and Edinburghers, will come nearer to understanding the essential Glasgow.

Albert Mackie

Abloa Under, beneath: **It's no fur me, postie, it's furra wumman in ra flet abloa.**

A

Abate I overcame: **He fancied he could come it owre me, but abate um in the en.**

Abettor Advisable action: **Abettor get aff ma mark.**

Abin Above: **Embruh claims tae be ra capital but Glesca stauns abin rum aw.**

Abloa Under, beneath: **It's no fur me, postie, it's furra wumman in ra flet abloa.**

Adzcreck That is correct.

Adze That is.

Aff Off, as in the historic cry of the Glasgow conductress before the days of one-man buses: **C'moan, get aff!**

Affa Off, or, off of: **Ye canny shuv yer granny affa bus.**

Affiliate A man devoured: **Ah laid aside a pie fur masell but affiliate it.**

Affy Off of: **Keep yer mine affy ra bevvy an attenty yer wife!**

Afore Previously, as in the sergeant's command to the platoon at drill: **Keep yer eyes in front, yizzuv saw me afore.**

Agane Opposed to: **Ra minister wiz preachin on adultery – he wiz agane it.**

Aheed In front: **He wiz aheed on pints – he goat knoaked oot, but.**

Ahin Behind: **Ach, ye're aye ahin like ra coo's tail.**

Alang Along: **Ah'll gie ye wan wirra heed an twaw wirra bunnet alang wi't.**

Alloo Permit: **Adze no allooed here.**

Alpaca Promise to fetch provisions: **Alpaca cuppla kerry-oots when Ah cum an see yiz.**

Amang Among: **See oor Wull? Iz aye amang ra talent.**

Ammonia Start of song beltit oot at many a pub door: **Ammonia stroalan vah-agga bawn. . .** It means also **I owe you**, as in **Ammonia cuppla quid arreddies, but.**

Amphora Expression of choice: **Amphora glessna pint** (If you twist my arm I shall accept a large whisky and a pint of heavy).

Analogy An habitual reaction: **Ah've goat analogy tae saft drinks.**

Anaw Also: **Ma farra's at ra dugs an ma brurra's err anaw**.

Andante With the addition of a female relative: **Muncle's err andante.**

Anerrits Immediate fulfilment of a promise: **Ah'll gie ye a slap on the jaw – anerrits!**

Argybargy A chow-the-rag, such as a debate on the District or Regional Cooncil.

Arise The mickey: **Ach, iz jiss takin arise ooty ye.**

Arra The missile from a boananarra; also, are the, as in **We arra people.**

Arreddies Already.

Artisses Entertainers in a working men's club, as exemplified in the chairman's remarks: **An lit me remine youse gents, artisses is nut dugs furty be whisselt at.**

Aseptic A disbeliever.

Aside Beside: **You're no awfy pernickety sittin aside ra likes o roan** (You are not very particular sitting beside such a person).

Assymetry A burial place such as the Necropolis.

Astray A wisp of dried grass which shows the way the wind is blowing.

At That; who; which.

Atom A reaction to a male person, or to persons: **Ah kin tell ye Ah'm ferr scunnert atom.**

Attacky case The *vade mecum* or *sine qua non* of the middle-class, professional gent or toff.

Attain I took, as in **Attain a ninsun dislike tae ur.**

Austere Invitation to all the company to participate in the preparation of a plum duff or Christmas pudding.

Avenue Change of plan: **Naw, hauf a meenit, avenue idea.**

Aw Everybody; all.

Awawn Avaunt, aroint thee, get lost: **Awawn scratch! Awawn bile yer heed! Awawn dunk yer doughnut!**

Awbdy Everybody: **Awbdy goat wan barn me** (Everybody got one except me).

Awrabest Farewell; heartiest good wishes.

Awraboays The gang.

Awragirra Altogether.

Awrasame Nevertheless.

Awratime All the time: **Here we are, awragirra, awragirra, awratime** (alleged Gaelic song taught to Ghurkas by Alec Finlay in the Far East).

B

Baccarat In the rear: See at fat flah in middle urra photey – Ah'm at ra baccarat.

Back The open space behind a tenement.

Bags I saw it first; also, an elegant sufficiency, sometimes expressed as **plennybags** and often as **bagsaplenny**.

Bait Dead tired.

Baith Both: **Nat applies tae baith ra three o yiz.**

Balloon A large, useless person – for instance, one's husband.

Bam Short for **bampot**.

Bambaized Perplexed, a strong mixture of bamboozled and amazed, usually **Clean bambaized**.

Bampot A head-case. Also, **bammer**.

Bamstick A useless person or thing, a wash-out, often applied to a stumer or duff tip at **ra dugs** or **Err races** (the Ayr meeting).

Banjo To clout over the head – for instance, one's husband.

Bap Breakfast roll.

Bapfittit Flat-footed, a term usually applied to 'ra polis'.

4

Baps Feet.

Barge Intrude.

Baritone Quality of singing reminiscent of a badly-oiled wheelbarrow.

Bar L. H.M. Prison, Barlinnie.

Barm Keep him out!

Barn Except: **Ra haill jingbang turnt up, barn Cherlie.**

Barra Barrow: **Awawn edger barra!** (Get out of my road!).

Barralan Glasgow's best-known landmark.

Barras An open-air market.

Barrel A disadvantageous position: **Sumdy's goat sumdy owrra barrel** (Someone has a certain person at a distinct disadvantage).

Bat Tennis racket: **We wid baith luv tae play tennis but we've went an furgoat wur bats.**

Batter Alcoholic bout: **Iz oan ra batter ivvry Setterday.**

Baurly A breathing-space.

Baw Ball, also a spree: **oan ra baw** (on the booze); **ra baw's oan ra slates** (the game is up).

Bawheed A big, useless person – in fact, 'a muckle sumph'.

Bean Brain (noun and transitive verb): **Awawn use yer bean, Jimmy!**; **His missis beaned um wirra purritch poat.'** But, **shuman bean** (*homo sapiens*).

Beldyheedit Lacking hair; also, recklessly: **He went at it beldyheedit.**

Bellusiz Bellows, used before central heating:
> **Kiltie, kiltie Calder**
> **couldny play a drum –**
> **His faither took the bellusiz**
> **An blew um up the lum.**

Ben Through the house: **Come ben an make yersell at hame!** It also means to bend.

Bender Alcoholic bout.

Benign Early: **Ah'll get banjoed if Ah'm no hame benign.**

Bent Crooked, usually applied to 'ra polis'.

Berd Beard.

Berdy A bearded person; a loach; a game Grampaw plays with the children, stroking their cheeks with his unshaven chin.

Berr Bare; bear; 'scuddy-nakit'.

Berry Rude noise made in the Glasgow Empire, reputed graveyard of English comedians.

Bevvy A drink or a trace of alcohol: **Ye could tell he had a bevvy oan um; If ye like Ah'll bring ye a bevvy; He'd be a nice flah if it wizny furra bevvy.**

Bias An unsubtle suggestion: **When ye gonny bias a bevvy?**

Bibulous Addicted to Bible study: **Ay, meenister, we're aw bibulous roon here.**

Bide Reside: **Adze whaur awra big poats bide.**

Bigamy Generous: **D'ye no hink it's bigamy tae staun ye a bevvy?**

Bigheed A person spoiled by success.

Bigot Someone who does not share one's prejudices.

Bike Alcoholic trip: **Keep yer eye oan um, iz oan iz bike.**

Bile Boil: **Awawn bile yer can!**

Bin To bind.

Bint A girl.

Birl Whirl.

Bit Boot: **Adze whan he stertit tae pit ra bit in**.

Bizarre A shopping centre or Christmas sale.

Bizzim A hussy, as well as a sweeping brush. Girls used to retort, when thus labelled:

> **A bizzim's a broom**
> **Fur sweepin a room**
> **An Ah'm a lady's daughter.**

Blaw To boast; a boaster.

Blawhard A person given to boasting.

Blew Blown **Ye've ferr blew the gaff noo, son**.

Blid Blood.

Bliddy Just about the most polite expletive, used along with others to improve the rhythm of the sentence.

Boa Boat, so spelt to convey the fact that the *t* is really a glottal stop. One vessel was humorously painted with the name *Raboa* (The Boat).

Boak To be sick: **Snuff tae gie ye ra boaks**.

Boa'ul Bottle: hereafter let it be understood that even a double *t* can be a glo'al stop.

Boay Lad: in plural, the gang: **wan urra boays**.

Boil The bile, as pronounced by those who wish to talk proper.

Bon Orchestra or band: **This French bint says, 'Scoatch soadger no bon,' an Ah says, 'Whit a cheek! Weers is ra best bon in ra British Army'.**

Bony Bonny. Check it up at the next pub chorus and you'll find she was '*bony* Annie Laurie'.

Book The betting record: **Ah axed ma owl man hoo he wiz daein, an he said he wiz beatin ra book.**

Boozer A bar.

Borra Trouble, bother: **nae borra** (no trouble – often 'spoke sarcastical').

Boss The wife.

Bounty Obliged to; certain to: **Yer bus is bounty be here in a cuppla meenits.**

Bowdie Bandy-legged.

Bowel A bowl: **The M.O. axed the cook 'How's your bowels?' and he says, 'Ma bowels is aw right but Ah'm shoarty a cuppla spins.'**

Bowlie See **bowdie.**

Brammer Something worthy of great praise: **See at new caur o his? Adze a brammer** (a beauty).

Breed Bread: **Ye ken fine Ah canny chuck ye doon a chit the noo – yer Paw's at the fitbaw wirra breed knife.** (You know well that I cannot throw you down a piece just now – Pater is at the match with the bread knife.)

Broon Brown.

Broonkaidies Bronchitis.

Bubblyjock Turkey-cock.

But However, used in Glasgow at the end of a sentence.

Butty Bosom friend.

Byke Wasps' nest.

Byne A washtub.

Bibulous Addicted to Bible study: **Ay, meenister, we're aw bibulous roon here.**

C

Cahootchy India rubber: **a man wi' a cahootchy neck**.

Cakey Ridiculous

Cakey Anna A ridiculous woman.

Cam Came: **Muncle cam fae Murrawell** (My uncle hied from Motherwell).

Camphor Object of mission: **Adze whit Ah camphor**.

Can Stupid person, dupe, pushover: **'Ah'm nut a can, Ah'm Dorothy Ann'** (old song by Dora Lindsay, comedienne of the Great War years).

Canny Careful; cannot: **ye canny be owre canny** (you can't be too careful).

Carkage A carcase.

Caul Cold: **Sawfy caul**.

Caulbliddit Cold-blooded.

Caulcreem Cold cream.

Caulhertit Cold-hearted.

Caulshoora To give someone the cold shoulder.

Caunle Candle: **He couldny haud a caunle tae ur**.

Caur Car.

Caution A comic: **He hud us aw in stitches: he wiz a right caution**.

Caw Call; drive; pull: **Awawn caw yer girr!** (Away and trundle your hoop!).

Champ Dancer Spooneristic rhyming slang for a 'damned chancer'.

Champers Teeth.

Chantyrassler A pretentious but insignificant person.

Chat A thingmejig or dingbat.

Chatty Personally unclean.

Chauvinist Wee Shuey (Big Aggie's Man).

Cheapjeck A market salesman; a grafter; a con-man.

Cheeny China: **Mine ma guid cheeny!** (Be careful with my good china).

Cheeryoppidist Person who improves life by manipulating feet: **It's nice tae think her serr feet are in the hauns o a weel-kent face** (Willie McCulloch).

Cheerypractor A chiropractor.

Cheeseperrin Niggardly.

Chep Native of Kelvingrove who eats Cantonese keery-oots under cover of his raincoat.

Chergesheet List of offences.

Cherr Chair: **Err a cherr owre err** (Yonder is a chair, over there).

Cherrity Something that begins at home: **as caul as cherrity**.

Cherrman Gentleman who presides over free-and-easy.

Cherrwumman Lady who presides over hen party.

Chimlay Chimney. Also known as **a lum**.

China One's friend, from 'china plate', rhyming slang for 'mate'.

Chinee Thought to be the singular of 'Chinese'.

Chips Some confusion here between **tottie chips** and the chips used in gambling: **Ye've hud yer chips**, and, **If Ah wiz yew, Ah'd chuck in ma chips**.

Chirp Bird call, used instead of a wolf whistle.

Chit A sandwich or other 'piece', carried to school or work, or thrown from a tenement window to an importunate child.

Chitter Shiver.

Chittery Chit A shivery bite – a sandwich or other edible object to be taken after bathing.

Choap The sack.

Choapper Redundancy action.

Chokefoo Filled to capacity: **Ra shoap's chokefooy folk**.

Choky The jail. Solitary confinement.

Chooky A pullet or hen.

Chow To chew food. **Chow the rag**, argue the point. **Chow the tartan**, speak Gaelic: **Ye should hear ra Heelanmen unner ra Heelanman's Umberella, chowan ra tartan.** (See **Heelanman**).

Chuch Tough: **chuch jeans**, a sweetmeat which involves much chewing.

Chuck Bread: **a daud o chuck**, a piece of bread. Also, to throw: **Ah wiz only in ra place five meenits whan Ah wiz chuckt oot; Chuck iz doon a daud o chuck, Maw!**

Chug Pull: **Ye'll need tae gie it anurra chug.**

Chum To convoy: **Ah'll chum ye hame; Whit aboot giein iz a chum?** (What about convoying me?)

Chute Now a device for disposing of rubbish in a tower block, but figuratively any slide to extinction: **Respeck fur owl age is aw doon ra chute noo.**

Chyne Chain: **Ah pooed ra chyne oan um, lang ago** (I gave him up a long time ago).

Chynge Change: **Ony-hing fur a chynge; Soarry, Ah've nae chynge; D'ye no hink it's time ye chynged yer sark?**

Chyngin Becoming effeminate, as if changing sex: **Jings, Ah hink iz chyngin** (Dear me, I think he is undergoing a sex change).

Cigrettekerd Card included in packet of cigarettes: anciently **cigrettephotey**.

Cinnermavis Rag-picker or ash-bucket raker.

Cinners Cinders.

Clabber Thick mud.

Clack Chatter: **Haud yer clack!** (Hold your tongue!).

Claes Clothes.

Claescloazit A wardrobe.

Claesline A rope for hanging clothes.

Claespeg A clothes peg; sometimes 'claespeen'.

Claivers Idle gossip.

Clappers Used in the expression: **Run like ra clappers**, to run at a terrific speed.

Clart Dirt; an untidy person.

Clarty Dirty; slovenly. Those who preferred the old tenement life used to declare: **The clartier the cosier** (The dirtier, the more livable).

Clash Talk; gossip. **Sterrheed clash** (what the neighbours are saying).

Clatter Hit; punish: **Ah'll clatter ye, ye wee bizzim.**

Claw Scratch. **Awawan claw!** (Go away and don't annoy me!).

Clean Adverb used to intensify meaning: **clean bambaized** (completely bamboozled); **clean bate** (completely exhausted); **clean aff-haun** (completely extempore).

Cleaners Bankruptcy: **Ra missis taen me tae ra cleaners.**

Clear Completely: **He's goat clear awaw wi't.**

Cleg A horsefly or gadfly (*tubanus bovinus*); an unpleasant fellow; a persistent nuisance, an income-tax inspector; a debt collector.

13

Clerty Tommy Morgan's signature phrase, a corruption of 'I declare to God!'

Click A piece of luck; a pick-up; to have luck.

Clippy A transport conductress in memorable days: **ra clippy wirra quippy** (the conductress with the repartee). Used in the song, **'She's jist a Kelty clippy, but Ah love her jist the same'**.

Cloak Clock: **Whit time is it? – It's fowr a cloak.**

Cloaker A cockroach or a broody hen.

Cloazit The loo.

Cloor Hit over the head: **Ah'll cloor ye.**

Cloot Cloth. **Flerr cloot** (floor cloth); **dish cloot** (dish cloth).

Clooty Dumplin Plum pudding boiled in a cloth.

Cludgie The loo.

Clumpers Feet.

Clype To inform.

Coaf Cough.

Coaffen A coffin: **It wiz a coaf at kerried um oaf; it wiz a coaffen they kerried um oaf in.** Also known as a **deedkist**.

Coak A cock; to cock: **Ye needny coak yer neb at me** (You need not cock your nose at me); also a term of endearment addressed to a small boy.

Coakabendy A comical wee man or boy.

Coakapenty Patronising.

Coaker A cocker spaniel.

Coakle A shellfish; the cockle.

Coakney A Londoner; in a London accent or style: **Ye needny come at Coakney stuff wi me** (It is useless to try to put over London tricks on me).

Coakynut Coconut: **That proves there's milk in ra coakynut.**

Coalic A pain in the stomach: **Deil coalic yer wame!** (May you suffer for it!).

Coalieshangay A dogfight, a disturbance.

Coalur Something worn round the neck; **dug's coalur,** a dog's or a minister's collar.

Coanfab A discussion; to discuss.

Coanfrince An important meeting.

Coanjestit Complicated; packed tightly.

Coanjoogles Marital rights.

Coanjurur A man who does tricks.

Coanman Any deceitful person.

Coansint Constant.

Coanstibble A policeman.

Coantack A coming together; to get in touch.

Coantrack An agreement: **It's no in ra coantrack.**

Coanturdickry Saying the opposite.

Coanturmashus Argumentative.

Coanvick An old lag.

Coanvickit Found guilty.

Coanvint A place where nuns reside or teach: **Ye widny hink she wiz ivver lernt in a coanvint, wid ye?**

Coanvirsashiony An old-fashioned tea-and-bun concert.

Coanvirsation A collogue.

Coarkscrew A man from Paisley, whose natives are believed always to carry one.

Coarn An irritating swelling on the feet; oats.

Coarnbeef Canned beef; deaf: **Ye'll need tae shout, he's coarnbeef.**

Coarnflooer Cornflower; cornflour.

Coarnry A heart attack.

Coarnur A corner kick at soccer.

Coarnurt Trapped.

Coarny Played-out – for instance, a joke or theatrical situation.

Coarp A corpse.

Coarprul A non-commissioned officer.

Coast Price: **It'll coast ye** (It will be pricey).

Code A codfish; a swindle; a con-man; to deceive: '**Whaw d'ye hink ye're codin?**' (Whom do you think you are deceiving?).

Coo A cow.

Coor To cower: **Ra wee dug's feert: iz coorin.**

Coordy A coward; a taunt to someone who refuses to join in.

Coortin Courtship.

Coory in Keep close!

Cooshydoo A wood pigeon; a term of endearment: **ma wee cooshydoo.**

Coozlick A quick, and not very complete, wash.

Cowp To capsize; a rubbish dump.

Crabbit Short-tempered.

Crack Conversation: **C'moan an geez yer crack!** (Come on and have a chat with me).

Craitur Creature, often used pityingly: **ra wee craitur.**

Crap it Give in prematurely; show the yellow streak.

Crapper A person who gives in; a boxer who takes a dive.

Craw A crow; to crow: **Ye needny craw sae croose** (You should not boast, you may be let down).

Create Make a fuss: **Noo dinny yew stert creatin!**

Crib To complain.

Croabrate Corroborate: **Ra cherge wiz nivver croabratit.**

Croak To murder; an aged cripple: **an aul croak.**

Croass To contradict, oppose.

Croasspatch A peevish child.

Croasstalk Rapid dialogue, joke and repartee.

Crony A pal; an old associate: **ra cronies** (the gang).

Crood Crowd.

Croods Cream cheese.

Croon To hit over the head.

Crucify To persecute: **Lass time Ah went tae Rouken Glen, ra midges wiz crucifyin' me**.

Cruelty The Royal Scottish Society for the Prevention of Cruelty to Children; an inspector from that organisation.

Crummle To disintegrate.

Cry To give a name to: **Whit ye gonny cry um?** (What name are you going to give him?).

Cuddy A donkey; a fool; a horse. **Ra cuddies** (horseracing).

Cumdoon A setback: a decline: **Whit a cumdoon!**

Curfuffle Disorder.

Curmurrin A rumbling in the stomach, otherwise known as **a wammlin wame**.

Curryhunkert Sitting on one's hams.

Cutty A short tobacco pipe, a clay pipe.

Chittery Chit A shivery bite – a sandwich or other edible object to be taken after bathing.

D

Dab Just what is required: **ra verra dab.**

Dabhaun An expert: **He wiz aye a dabhaun at derts.**

Daddy The best: **Oor Wull is ra daddy urrum aw** (Our William is the best of them all).

Dae To do: **Ah get fed up wi nuh-hin tae dae** (I am bored when I have nothing to do).

Dae awaw Carry on; render redundant; kill: **They're gonny dae awaw wi hauf the wurkers.**

Dae doon Cheat.

Dae fur Kill: **Ah'll dae fur um afore Ah'm feenisht.**

Dae in Exterminate: **As sherr as daith, Ah'll dae that laddie in yit.**

Dae ooty Cheat of a right: **They're tryin tae dae us ooty it.**

Dae up Decorate: **Ye take that lang tae dae yersell up.** Also maim: **Ra boays thraitent tae dae um up if he cam back.**

Dae wioot Get on despite the lack: **We lernt tae dae wioot it.**

Daft Silly.

Daftie A silly person.

Daidlie An apron.

Daisent Decent; adequately clothed: **Ye're no daisent** (You are over-exposed).

Daisychyne A chain composed of daisies.

Daith Death: **as fack's daith** (as true as death); **Ye'll get yer daith o caul** (You will perish with the cold).

Dannylion Dandelion; traffic warden.

Darg A stint at work.

Dawby A stupid person.

Debaur To exclude.

Deckcherr A collapsible seat of canvas and light wood or metal.

Deckhaun A member of the ship's crew.

Deckhoose A house on the deck of a ship.

Declerr Reveal to the Customs: **nuh-hin tae declerr** (nothing to declare).

Dedication Something Andy Cameron does on Radio Scotland.

Deed Passed away.

Deedbait Absolutely exhausted.

Deedcenner Right in the middle of the target.

Deeden To render numb.

Deed enn A stop; the finish: **We've cum tae a deed enn**.

Deedloak A complete standstill, especially in an industrial dispute.

Deedthraws The last spasms: **We are witnessin ra deedthraws urra capittalist system**.

Deffinly Deafeningly or definitely.

Dekko An inspection; a good look, a close examination: **Hae a dekko at that wan**.

Dementit Up the wall: **Yiz'll drive me dementit**.

Denizen Dennistoun.

Dennal To do with teeth: **Iz a dennal surgeon**.

Denner Lunch: **It wiz wan o thae hotels whaur ye get lunch fur yer denner and denner fur yer tea**.

Dennist A person who cares for the teeth.

Derken Cast a shadow over: **The funeral proceedins wiz derkent be the news that the Rangers had goat bait**.

Dern Daring.

Derrimennal Bad for: **Noo they're sayin smokin's derrimennal tae yer health**.

Derry A place where milk, cheese and butter are produced.

Derryferm A cattle farm.

Derrymaid A young woman who works on a dairy farm.

Derts The game of darts.

19

Desertspin A spoon used for the sweet course.

Deserves Serves, in the phrase, **It deserves ye right!**

Dessnation Place for which one is headed.

Dessny Fate; kismet.

Desstute On one's uppers.

Deteck Discover; apprehend: **Dae yew deteck a smell?**

Deteeriate Get worse.

Determint Resolved; unshakeable: **Ye're that determint.**

Dibs Remuneration for work; wealth: **He's goat ra dibs.**

Dicky Starched shirt front, or a substitute for it: **Awra toffs wiz there wi their dickies oan.**

Did Done: **See whit ye've went an did.**

Dike A wall between backs.

Ding To hit hard; to ring: **Gie ra bell a ding.**

Discoont Something off the price.

Disenchannit Awakened to the realities of life.

Dishcloot A cloth for washing dishes.

Dishtool A cloth for drying dishes.

Dishwatter A criticism of certain beers.

Disjynit Incoherent.

Dissrick An area: **Dissrick Cooncil** (the local authority).

Distrackit With one's attention drawn away.

Dlibbrit Intentional: **Sich an oaffer is a dlibbrit insult.**

Dlinquent An offender against the law.

Dlivver Carry purchases to the purchaser.

Dlootit Of a liquid, made weaker by the addition of water — for instance, beer, whisky or milk.

Doddle A walkover in work or sport: **It's a doddle.**

Doge A trick.

Doll Mode of address to a lady by a bus driver.

Done Did.

Donner A short walk; to wander.

Donnert Stupid.

Doo Pigeon.

Dook To bathe; a swim: **Ah'm aff furra dook, well.**

Doolander A man's cap or Scotch bonnet, on which pigeons are imagined as landing.

Doon Down.

Doonfaw Sudden descent, or the cause of it: **Adze been iz doonfaw.**

Doonhertit Jaded.

Doonpoor A deluge.

Doonrawatter A sail down the Clyde Estuary.

Doonsterrs On a lower floor.

Doorpost Repository of secrets: **atween yew nye na doorpost.**

Doot To suspect. **Ah doot it'll rain** means the opposite of 'I doubt it will rain' in Southern English or American.

Doots Uncertainty: **Ah hae ma doots** (I am unsure, but I suspect).

Dour Severe: **He wiz aye a dour customer.**

Dowp A cigarette end; a backside.

Doze Spin: **Awawn doze yer peerie!** (Away and spin your top!).

Dozy Stupid; inefficient.

Dreep Drip; a soft, inefficient person; to drop from a wall: **Ah jiss hud tae dreep ra dike.**

Drew Drawn: **Ah huvny drew ma wages yit.**

Drook To soak.

Drookin A severe wetting.

Drooth Drought; thirst; a heavy drinker.

Dub A pool of water: **Juck dub** (a duck pond); **'Goose Dubs'**, an old Glasgow placename.

Duds Old clothes: **Thaim's no ma warkin duds.**

Dug A dog.

Dughoose Trouble; 'Coventry': **Ah'm in ra dughoose at hame.**

Dugmatic Said of someone who tends to disagree with one.

Dugsbrekfist A mess.

Dugsflurrish A white wayside flower.

Dugtyert Exhausted.

Dumfoonert Dumbfounded.

Dung Beaten; hit; **dung oot** (exhausted).

Dunkies' ages A long time: **Ah huvny saw ye fur dunkies' ages.**

Dunky An ass.

Dunkywark The least pleasant but most essential part of any operation: **Ah've did ra dunkywark: get oan wi't!**

Dunny Back lobby in a close.

Dusskerrt Cart for collecting refuse.

Dux Top of the class: **Go up dux!** (That's clever of you).

Dwaiblie Not looking or feeling very well; physically weak.

Dwinnleshanks Skinny and unsteady legs.

Dyleck The funny way they speak in Paisley.

Dylectic Rudiments of the situation, as explained by a comrade.

E

Edge Move: **Edge yer barra, Jimmy!** (Get out of the way).

Effeck Meaning: **He tellt me tae get loast, or words tae that effeck.**

Eleck Choose.

Elky One's mark, after boxer Elky Clark: **Ah goat aff ma Elky.**

Emoashnal Angry: **There's nae need tae stert gettin emoashnal aboot it.**

Empooert Given authority: **Ah propose that wur saicretry be empooert furty write a stinkin letter.**

Emral Green, used almost exclusively of the **Emral Isle.**

Enammert In favour: **Adze sum-hing Ah nivver wiz enammert wi.**

Encase Supposing: **Ah didny expeck trouble, Ah jiss took a brick alang encase, but.**

Enema The end of my: **Ah'm at ra enema patience.**

Enemy The time, especially when it approaches closing time.

Enn The finish; to bring to a close.

Enncoar A performance brought on after the 'enn'; **Ah hink ra surgeon took oot ma appennix fur an enncoar.**

Err In that direction: **Err itz owre err** (There it is over there); **Errzarerrperrahochs** (There is a young lady with rather a fetching pair of legs).

Exackly Precisely.

Exasprit Annoy: **Awawn no exasprit me!**

Exemp Excused duty.

Exratressral Out of this world.

Extenn Stretch.

Extink No longer available.

Exyumed Disinterred.

Exzaustit At the end of one's tether.

Exzibbitit Showed.

23

F

Face Confront: **Less face it!**

Facecloot A cloth with which to wash the face.

Faceliff Plastic surgery: **She wiz huvvin her face liftit whan the crane broke.**

Fack Something indisputable: **Ah walked away an said, Izzat a fack?; zamarrafack** (as a matter of fact).

Fae From.

Fancy Estimate: **Ye ferr fancy yer chance** (You have a good opinion of yourself).

Fancyman Paramour.

Fantoosh Elaborately decorative; fancy.

Farnlaw Spouse's father.

Farnmurra One's parents (same as Pawnmaw).

Farra Father: **Ra man hit ra boay though he wizny his farra.**

Fascist The gaffer.

Fash Trouble: **Dinny fash yersel, hen!** (Do not worry, lady).

Fashus Over-anxious.

Fat-heed A stupid person; **Fat-heedit** (rather dense).

Fatloat Much (sarcastic): **A fatloat yew kerr** (Little you care).

Fatralaun Comfort and prosperity: **He's livin oan ra fatralaun.**

Fatsnafire Crisis: **Ra fatsnafire noo, well.**

Faut Blame: **Sno ma faut** (I am not to blame); **Ach, ye're aye finnan faut wimmy.**

Favour Used in the phrase **froany favour** (for goodness sake).

Febbyurry The month of February.

Feckless Not much use; unable to cope.

Feed Nourishment, intake of food: **Ah'm aff ma feed** (I am unable to eat).

Feerdie A coward.

Feerdiegowk The same.

Feert Frightened.

Fell Fallen: **Dinny tell me ye've went an fell again?; Get fell in, youse!**

Fernietickles Freckles.

Ferr Fare: **Ferrs, please!; Whitsaferr?** (What is the fare?). Also fair; the Glasgow Fair Holidays.

Ferra Feather: **They're jiss birds o a ferra.**

Ferrabed A soft lie.

Ferraweight Small jockey or boxer.

Ferrherd Blond.

Ferrnsquerr Above-board, on the level.

Ferry A creature of the other world.

Ferrystory A false rumour.

Ferrytale A fib.

Fift Round 5: **He done a tank job in ra fift** (He took a dive in the fifth round).

File To soil: **Ah widny file ma hauns oan um.**

Fill Enough: **Ah've hud ma fill o that wan.**

Fillum A moving picture.

Fillumstaur An idol of the screen: **He fancies hiz-sell as if he wiz a fillumstaur.**

Fin Find; feel: **Here, Ah fin a funny smell**.

Finance Boyfriend.

Fine hamahaddie Sarcastic response to an excuse (literally, trying to pass haddock off as ham).

Fine ye ken Do not try to pretend ignorance.

Firedug An andiron.

Firegerrd A shield on a fire, a fire watcher.

Firewid Wood to start a fire.

Fishile Oil obtained from fish.

Fishinteckle Requisites for the sport of angling.

Fit The pedal extremity: **Ah've a serr fit** (My foot aches).

Fitbaw The game of soccer; the ball used in it.

Fithaud A safe place on which to place the foot in climbing.

Fitserr Weary of walking or dancing; footsore.

Fizzy drink Champagne, Asti Spumante, or other irritatit watter.

Flakjeckit Soldier's tunic.

Flamin Mild expletive used in mixed company.

Flatry Praise with an ulterior motive: **Flatry'll no get ye naeplace.**

Flerr Floor: **err – oana flerr** (there – on the floor); **Flerrcloot** (cloth used to wash floors).

Flerrpoalish Wax employed in giving a shine to a floor.

Flet A saucer; a floor level; an apartment; flat:
Murder, murder, polis, three sterrs up,
ra wumman oana toap flet hut me wi a cup.

Fletten To lay low: **Awaw or Ah'll fletten ye!**

Flew Flown: **Ye're owre late – ra bird's flew.**

Flewr Flour; flower: **'Jessie ra flewry Dumblane'.**

Flewry Flowery; floury; nickname for a baker or someone with the surname Baker.

Flewryscennit Fluorescent.

Fly Cunning; **Flyman** (a con-man or plain crook).

Foalyer Someone who shadows a person; a disciple.

Foons The foundations.

Foontain A fountain; a street well.

Footer To hesitate; a person who finds difficulty in deciding.

Forehaunit Paid in advance, such as rent or rates.

Foreheed The brow.

Fowr Four.

Fowrfittit Quadruped.

Fowrnhaun A carriage drawn by four horses.

Frankenstein The gaffer.

Freen A relative; a friend: **She's nae freen o mine** (She is not a friend, or, she is not related to me).

Frichtit Scared: **Gaun! Whit are ye frichtit at?** (Go ahead: what are you afraid of?).

Froak A woman's dress.

Froon To scowl: a wrinkled brow; to disapprove.

Fun Found: **Ye luck as if ye've fun a fiver.**

Furgerra Forget her; forgather.

Furrit Forward: **Pit yer bess fit furrit!**

Fursscless Excellent.

Furssfit The visitor who first crosses the threshold at New Year.

Furss-haun Of information, straight from the horse's mouth.

Furssly In the first place.

Furssrate Of supreme quality.

Furty In order to; used to introduce the infinitive: **Ra coamitee hiz decidit furty chynge ra venue fae ra Tuesday tae ra Friday.**

G

Gadaboot A person who flits from place to place; to run around.

Gaff A secret; **blawra gaff** (let the cat out of the bag).

Galavantan Doing the town.

Gallus Devil-may-care: **Here, yew're no hauf gallus.**

Galoshans Overshoes; 'Galatians', a New Year guisers' play.

Gammyleggit With a game leg; dot and carry one.

Gamutt The entire range of anything: **He went through the haill gamutt.**

Gander A look: **Naw, Ah'm no inrestit, Ah'm jiss haein a gander.**

Gangwey Kindly get out of the road and let me pass!

Garret The maiden's doom:
> An' it's oh, dear me,
> Whit will Ah dae
> If Ah dee an aul maid in a garret?

Gas Impudence: **Less o yer gas, noo!**; **Ah shin pit his gas in a peep.**

Gasbag That wumman next door.

Gaun Going.

Gaur Make, cause to: **Dinny gaur me belt ye wan!**

Gawnyersell Cry of encouragement to a performer, especially a singer belting it oot or giving it 'laldy'.

Gerrit Comprehend: **Ah doan gerrit** (I do not follow your argument; I don't understand what is going on).

Gers Affectionate term for Rangers FC. Handy for sub-editors.

Getaboot To be able to move around town.

Getalang To accommodate oneself: **Hoo d'ye getalang wi yoan yin?**

Getawawwi Escape punishment: **Some folk getawawwi murder.**

Getoanty Scold: **Ye dinny need tae aye getoanty me.**

Getooty Avoid; escape the consequences: **Ye'll be lucky if ye getooty this wan.**

Getragirra To forgather; a meeting: **Ah'm aw fur a graun getragirra.**

Getroon Coax: **She's carnaptious but she's easy tae getroon.**

Ghee Give: **Dinny ghee me awaw!; Ah ghee in; Ah ghee up; Ghee owre!** (Desist!).

Gheed Past tense of ghee: **Ah gheed um a piecy ma mine** (I gave him a talking to); given: **Ah hink he's gheed up the ghost.**

Gheemizheed Let him get going; give him enough rope to hang himself.

Gheen Given; also ungrammatical but frequent for 'gave': **She ferr gheen it laldy** (She fairly gave the song gusto).

Girdlescoan A scone made on a griddle.

Girn Complain: **Whit d'ye keep girnan at, but?**

Gitter A bumbling person.

Gled Happy: **Ah'm aye gled tae see ye.**

Gledden To gladden: **Ra score gleddent ra herts o us aw.**

Gleg Smart.

Glerr Glare: **Ah canny staun ra glerr urra flewryscennit lights.**

Glerran Obvious: **It wiz a glerran penalty.**

Gless Glass: **Ye kin tell iz gless eye be the kind look in it.**

Glesshoose A hothouse or glazed house for rearing plants.

Glessie A glass 'bool' used in the game of 'bools' (marbles).

Gless jaw An inability to stand up to a sound punch, attributed to many a 'mug' boxer.

Gloamin The twilight: condition of light suitable for the romantic stroll by the bonnie banks of Clyde.

Glorious Blind-drunk.

Gnat Etcetera: **We'll be haein beer, gnat, an lager, gnat, an whisky, gnat, an mebbies sannitches, gnat.**

Goad A pious exclamation.

Goadfarra A male friend who witnesses a christening.

Goadmurra The female equivalent of a **goadfarra**.

Goaldigger A blonde out for one's money.

Goalplatit Plated with gold.

Goalrush A stampede for something attractive.

Goash An expletive of the more refined type.

Goaspel The absolute truth: **An adza goaspel Ah'm tellin ye.**

Goat Obtained: **He goat ma goat** (He annoyed me). Also, a fool: **Stoap ackin the goat!** (Don't carry on like a fool!).

Goonie Nightgown.

Goon show A mannequin parade.

Gowk A cuckoo; a fool; a dupe on April Fool's Day: **Magowk!** (April Fool!).

Grafter Hard worker; kerb salesman.

Graivel Wee chuckies (stones).

Grajate Finish with a degree at a university or college: **Av coorse, Ah grajatit wi oaners in English.**

Grammar Grandmother.

Gramp, grampaw Grandad.

Granfarra Polite form of **Grampaw**.

Greencheese A coveted object: **Ye canny see greencheese but yer een reels** (your eyes reel).

Greet To weep.

Greetinfaist One who is always complaining.

Griff Inside, authentic information: **Whitza griff, mac?**

Grubber Hard worker; the canteen; the jail.

Grubstake To pay for one's food or, more usually, drink.

Gruesome Grown somewhat: **Jings, at rhubart's gruesome.**

Grumf A disgruntled, complaining person.

Grumfy Epithet applied to a carnaptious old person.

Grun Ground: **Ah've nae gruns fur complaint; Ah like a flah
at's doon tae ra grun.**

Grunflerr The ground floor: **Ah like tae get in oana grunflerr.**

Guerre The guard.

Guerreroom Military jail.

Guess-hoose Bed and breakfast.

Guid Good (rhymes with *did*).

Guiddlegoadle Good Heavens!

Guidnaiturt Friendly and unperturbable.

Guidman Husband.

Guidness me A mild expletive.

Guidwife The lady of the house.

Guidwill The value of a shop, over and above stock.

Guidyoomert Easygoing.

Guiser A Hallowe'en or Hogmanay mummer: **Pleasty help ra
guisers!**

Guitar A persistent cold in the head.

Gully A large knife; a challenge to fight: **Gheem ra gully!**

Gumbile A swelling caused by bad teeth.

Gumbits Wellington boots, also known as **Wellies**.

Gunkerridge A wheel-carriage for the transport of cannon.

Gunpoora Gunpowder.

Gurly Stormy, especially applied to the sea or a stream.

Gushet-nyuk A corner where two streets converge.

Gutties Rubber shoes.

H

Habitchate Accustom: **Ye shin get habitchatit tae ra wark** (You soon become accustomed to the work).

Habitchul Regular, addicted: **He's a habitchul sook** (He is a regular sycophant).

Habnab Hobnob, mix.

Haddie Haddock, as in **Finnan haddie, caller haddie** (fresh haddock).

Hag That wumman next door.

Haggis Undefinable.

Hagiology The study of haggis.

Hagioscope An instrument for examining haggis.

Haill Entire: **Ah'll shin soart ra haill jingbang o yiz** (I will soon deal with the entire gang of you).

Hailstanes A storm of hail: **Thae wur hailstanes as shuge as caussays** (There were hailstones as large as carriageway setts).

Hally een All Hallows' Eve.

Hamahaddie An expression of scepticism about pretensions or excuses: See **fine hamahaddie.**

Hame One's habitation, past or present: **See Sammy – Ah hink he's packed up and went hame.**

Hamish James (from Gaelic **Sheumais**).

Hap Wrap: **Ye'll better hap yersell up, it's gettin caul.**

Hapny Halfpenny, preserved in the mysterious saying, **Keep yer haun oan yer hapny!** (Protect yourself!).

Harl Roughcast applied to outside walls.

Hatpeen A pin for keeping a lady's hat on; also, a handy weapon against muggers.

Hauf A small whisky, a nip.

Haufback A footballer playing in midfield.

Haufbrurra A brother by one parent only.

Hauf-coak Like a gun not completely cocked: **Ye've jiss went aff hauf-coak** (You have simply started to fulminate before fully appreciating the situation).

Hauf-deed Condition the morning after the night before.

Hauf-hertit Unenthusiastic in action.

Hauf-hoaliday A half-day off.

Hauf-mast Hanging low: **His troozers is aye hauf-mast.**

Hauf-nelson An effective wrestling hold: **Ah'll shin pit ra hauf-nelson oan ra likes o yew** (I will soon deal with your sort).

Hauf seas owre Becoming tipsy.

Haufwey Midway.

Haufwit The gaffer.

Haun Hand (noun and verb): **Haun me owre at chisel; Ah like ma femly nearhaun; Ye kin tell iz an aul haun be ra smeddum he pits intae his wark** (You can tell he is an old hand by the energy he puts into his work); **Ra perra rum's haun in glove ragirra** (The pair of them are hand in glove together); **At lad's gettin oota haun** (That boy is becoming impossible to control).

Haunanfit Hand and foot.

Haunbag A lady's portable receptacle.

Haungrup A hold for the hand; the strength of one's hand.

Haunkert A barrow; a cart propelled by hand.

Haunle To handle; handle: **'Mister', please! Ah've a haunle tae ma name same as awbdy else** (Remember to call me 'Mister'. I am entitled to it the same as others).

Haunlebaurs The steering hold on a bicycle; a large moustache.

Haun o write Handwriting: **Ah ken um be his haun o write.**

Haur Hard: **Dinny be sae haur oan um** (Don't be so hard on the boy); **He's haur-pit tae fin an excuse.**

Hauraheerin Deaf.

Haurbylt Hard-boiled, of an egg or a person.

Haurfaced With a tough and callous aspect.

Haurheedit Ultra-sensible, not easy to better in a bargain.

Haurhertit Immovable by emotional appeals.

Haur labour A spell in the Bar L.

Haurly Scarcely.

Haurman A gangster; a tough.

Haur tack Ship's biscuit; works canteen food.

Haw Hullo! **Haw Wull!** (Hullo, Willie, which became the name of a cartoon character representing the typical Glasgow man).

Hawk A hack, usually from frost.

Hawss Neck; throat: **Get that owre yer hawss!** (Drink it!).

Heed The head: to hit with the head (a football or a person).

Heed case An eccentric.

Heeder The action of striking the football with the head.

Heedit Destined: **Yoan yin's heedit fur trouble.**

Heedlamps Spectacles: **Ah didny ken ye wi thae heedlamps oan.**

Heedmaister The head of the school, now known as head teacher.

Heed-oan Frontal, in a collision or a confrontation.

Hedge A street trader's audience: **fanny ra hedge** (keep the crowd interested).

Heefer A bulky person.

Hee-haw Absolutely nothing; a let-down: **Whit did at guy ghee ye? – Hee-haw!**

Heelan Pertaining to the Highlands.

Heelanman A Highlander. **Ra Heelanman's Umberella** is the part of Argyle Street under the railway bridge where Highlanders and other exiles met together in the evenings and at weekends, especially in inclement weather.

Heelsowrgowdie Head over heels.

Heelytrope A light purple colour: **His face went heelytrope.**

Hell Very fast, in the expression **like the hammers o hell**; sometimes curtailed to **like the hammers**.

Hen Term of endearment addressed to a girl or a woman. Usually well-intentioned, but often giving offence to the uninitiated.

Henhoose Meeting place for females.

Hensperrty A get-together of the womenfolk; mothers' meeting.

Hen-taed In-toed.

Hereaboot In this locality.

Hereawaw In this direction.

Herm Injury: **At dug'll no dae ye nae herm**.

Hermless Just stupid; innocent.

Herp Keep repeating a complaint; **Dinny herp oan aboot it!**

Herr Hair: **She's no rat bony but ur herr's rerr** (She is not particularly good-looking but she has good hair); **Keep yer herr oan, Jimmy!**; **Ah nivver turnt a herr**; **Dinny yew stert splittin herrs!**.

Herrbrush A brush used for the hair.

Herrcloot A piece of cloth used as a hair curler.

Herrile Oil applied to the hair.

Herrnet A net to keep the hair in place, as worn by Ena Sharples.

Herrpeen Sometimes **herrpreen**, a pin to hold the hair in place.

Herrumskerrum Flighty.

Herry In the Twenties and Thirties, applied to a woman or girl who never wore a hat, referred to in the folk song, **Herry Merry an ra haurman** (Hatless Mary and the hoodlum).

Hersell Sometimes **ursell**, herself; on her own: **She's in hersell** (She is alone).

Hert The heart.

Hertbrek Anything that gets one down.

Hertburn Indigestion.

Hertless Cruel.

Hertseek Completely fed-up.

Herty Generous, often used sarcastically of a mean person: **Iz herty when he laughs**.

Hervest The gatherin-in of the fruit.

Hey Dried grass.

Heystack A stack of dried grass: **She'd a heeda herr like a heystack** (She had a hair-do that resembled a haystack).

Hiccup The latest euphemism for an industrial dispute.

Highdays Special occasions; as in **It's only oan highdays an hoalidays**.

Hin At the back.

Hindoo The last pigeon in a race.

Hing A thing: **An anurra hing!** (And another thing); to hang, as in the old tenement custom of **hingan oot ra windae wi ma elbaes in ma hauns**.

Hingaboot Loaf.

Hingoot To frequent: **Whaur dae yew hingoot?**

Hingragirra To maintain the principle of solidarity.

Hinguroan An acolyte or disciple; also just a moocher.

Hingyerheed Be ashamed: **Ye should hingyerheed in black burnan shame.**

Hink To think: **Whit d'ye hink o Mrs Thatcher?**

Hinleg Hind leg.

Hinmist The farthest back; the last: **Deil tak the hinmist!**

Hinnenn Finale: **It'll be aw the same at the hinnen.**

His-sell Himself; on his own: **Is the aul man at hame? – Ay, iz in his-sell.**

Hitramiss Haphazard.

Hoarse A member of the equine species.

Hoarseback Mounted.

Hoarseboax A carrier for horses.

Hoarsecoper A man who deals in horses; a con-man.

Hoarseherr Horse-hair.

Hoarsy man A man addicted to gambling on horse-racing.

Hoo In what manner?

Hooivver However.

Hoolet An owl.

Hoose A house.

Hoosebrecker A burglar.

Hooseprood Houseproud.

Hoosewife A housewife.

Hoosnhame House and home.

Hoosnhaud House and hold: **Ye'll eat iz ooty hoosnhaud** (You will eat me out of house and hold).

Hoozawwiye How are you?

Hoozyersell How are you; yourself? **The King asked, 'Who are you?' an Ah said, 'Fine, thank-ye, hoozyersell?'**

Howdie Midwife.

Hullawrerr Hullo there; cordial greeting.

Humf To carry a heavy load: **Ah kent um whan he humft coal** (I knew him when he was a coal-heaver).

Humfybackit Afflicted with a humped back; round-shouldered.

Hunkers Haunches: **Hunker doon!** (Sit down on the back of one's thighs).

Hurdies Buttocks; hips.

Hurl A lift on a vehicle, a short trip: in the old song, **Ah loast ma hurl oan ra barra** (I lost my ride on the barrow).

Hushion A stocking without feet, mentioned in Burns's song, **'Willie Wastle': She dichts her grunyie wi a hushion** (She wipes her face with a stocking).

Hyena An immoderate and annoying laugher.

I

Idennical Like, in every respect.

Idennify To pick out someone on an identification parade.

Idennity Identity.

Ile Oil: **Ah hink Ah've struck ile at last.**

Ilecan A container for oil.

Iled Lubricated: **He wiz weel-iled** (He was drunk).

Ilepentin Portrait in oils; **She's nae ilepentin, ye muss admit.**

Ileshoap Shop that sells oil.

Illegible Fit to be chosen: **the maist illegible bachelor in Maryhill.**

Illnaiturt Bad-tempered.

Illtreatit Abused.

Illwull Spite: **It's no at Ah berr um oany illwull: Ah jiss canny stick um.**

Illyaized Badly treated.

Imbrication Wintergreen or similar rubbing-oil used by athletes.

Immanent High up in the social scale: **He's quite an immanent flah, ken?**

Immigrate Emigrate: **Ah hink iz went an immigratit tae England.**

Impack Collision.

Imparadise At Celtic Park football ground.

Impartial Not caring who beats Celtic (or Rangers, as the case may be).

Impeccable Steadfastly refusing to be hen-pecked.

Impediment Habitual slowness in standing a round.

Imperr To damage.

Impetchis Rash; headlong; unthinking.

Impoassible Not capable of being performed.

Impotent Cheeky.

Income An ulcer.

Increck Quite erroneous.

Indreck In a roundabout manner.

Infamy Spite: **Ra polis hiz aye hud it infamy**.

Infeckit Of a wound, rendered worse by contact.

Injeck To force fluid in, by means of a syringe or pump.

Injeckit Introduced into the system.

Injin Native of India or aboriginal of the Americas.

Injin file One-by-one in procession.

Injyrubber See **cahootchy**.

Innernashnul A football match between Scotland and another country.

Innerprize Initiative: **Ra trouble wi yew is ye've no goat nae innerprize**.

Innerval Time to go out for a drink.

Innylecshul Gifted with brains and education.

Inreduction Presentation of one person to another.

Insanoots The complexities of a situation.

Inseck A person not worth considering.

Inside Spending a term in the Bar L.

Inspeck To examine carefully.

Insteed In place of: **Ah wiz hinkin o gaun tae ra picters, but Ah went tae ra boozer insteed**.

Instink Intuition.

Intack Entire; undiminished.

Intenn To purpose: **Ah didny intenn furty dae it**.

Interment Imprisonment.

Interrupter Person who translates a speech in a foreign language, in a law court.

Intit Isn't it?

Inty Into; isn't he?

41

Invite An invitation.

Ishy The main point of an argument.

Itsell Emphatic form of 'it'; itself.

Ivver At any time.

Ivvrybuddy All of us.

Iz Is; he is; his.

Izny Is not.

Iz-sell Himself: **He tellt me iz-sell.**

Izzy Is he? **Izzy in? – Naw, iz oot.**

Impeccable Steadfastly refusing to be hen-pecked.

J

Jabber Speak foreign, or posh.

Jake The knave in a suit of playing cards; methylated spirits as a drink.

Jalooze To suspect.

Jammy Lucky.

Jane Of a girl, shy and innocent: **a jane tart** (a good-living girl).

Jap A splash. The late Tommy Morgan said the armoured cars we used in the Far East had to have big mudguards 'tae keep the Japs aff'.

Jawboax The kitchen sink, or bathroom or bedroom hand-basin.

Jawhole A drain.

Jazzer A person addicted to frequenting dance halls.

Jeely Jelly or jam.

Jeelyfish A Portuguese man-o'-war, for instance.

Jeely nose A bloody proboscis.

Jeely piece The Scottish equivalent of Ken Dodd's 'jam buttie' (a jam sandwich), often thrown in the past from a tenement window to a child playing outside.

Jessy An effeminate man: **Awaw, yuh big Jessy!**

Jimmy Reid Rhyming slang for **heed** (head): **Use yer Jimmy Reid, Mac!**

Jink To avoid, for instance, 'ra polis'; also, Do you think?: **Jink iz goat much chance o gettin aff?** (Do you think he is very likely to be acquitted?).

Jinky A dodger; do you think of? **Whit jinky his chances?**

Jiss, Jist Only; barely: **Here, it's jiss occurt tae me. . .**

Joab A piece of work: **a guid joab** (fortunately).

Joaggernut A person who is crazy on jogging.

Joat An iota: **no a joat.**

Joaters The sack: one's 'books'.

Joker A fellow: **It wiz anurra joker awragirra** (It was a different person entirely).

Jokoh Unconcerned, unperturbed: **He jiss sat there, quite jokoh.**

Joogler A juggler, conjurer or twister.

Jyle Jail; police cell: **Here, yew'll get the jyle.**

Jyne Join.

Jyner Man who joins a drinking party in the hope of obtaining a drink and with no intention of paying his round; a carpenter.

Jynt Joint: **It's aw oot o jynt** (It is completely dislocated).

Jysts The parallel timbers between floors.

K

Kail Greens; Scotch broth: **caul kail het again** (an old story, or a sermon oft-repeated.)

Kailyerrd Cabbage patch.

Keek Peep, look: **Gheez a wee keek at yer paper, mac** (Kindly permit me to read your newspaper for a moment).

Keeker A black eye.

Keelhaulin A telling-off.

Keelie Someone from another street.

Keepaffy Abstain from: **Keepaffy ra naphthy** (Keep off the whisky).

Kennle To set alight.

Kent Knew, known: **Ah've kent it aw alang** (I have known it all the time).

Kern Being concerned about anything: **Ah'm jiss no kern** (I simply don't care).

Kerr To care: **If ye kerr aboot me ataw, ye'll no go.**

Kerrt A lorry or cart; to carry.

Kerrtit Taken away in a hearse: **Ye'll no get daein it till Ah'm kerrtit.**

Kickaff Opening of a game of soccer.

Kidmaleerie A fake.

Kidnapper One who tries to get off with a much younger member of the opposite sex.

Kidneys Deceiving me; teasing me: **Och, ye're jiss kidneys.**

Kill A hearty laugh: **They were ferr gettin their kill at ye.**

Kilt Killed; enjoyed: **He ferr kilt iz-sell whan he saw ur.**

Kin Can (emphatic): **Ye canny believe it, kin ye? – Ay, Ah kin.**

Kinny Sort of: **It's kinny caul, intit?; D'yew feel a kinny smell?**

Kist Chest; trunk; box; coffin.

Kistit Coffined.

Kitchen Something cooked, or dipped in dripping: **Ma man aye hiz tae hae kitchen tae his purritch** (My husband insists on something cooked after his porridge).

Kite Abdomen, especially an enlarged one: **Ye kin tell beez kite iz aye oan ra beer** (You can easily see by his bulging stomach that he is always drinking beer).

Kittle To tickle: **Diz that no kittle yer fancy?**

Knacker An old horse; a bad bet in a horse race.

Knackert Exhausted: **Ah'm no foo – Ah'm jiss knackert.**

Knew Known: **Ah've knew that fae the stert** (I have been aware of that fact from the beginning).

Knoakitaff Stop!

L

Laldy Gusto in singing: **She's no hauf giein it laldy** (She is fairly belting it out).

Lang Long: **He wiz a lang lunky a flah** (He was a long-bodied lizard of a man).

Langheedit Shrewd.

Langweys Lengthwise.

Langwinnit Boring, not knowing when to stop talking.

Larry Lorry.

Lashins Plenty.

Launry A place where clothes and bed linen are washed.

Lavner A sweet-smelling plant and the perfume made from it.

Lawcoort Place where law cases are heard.

Lawn Land: **He aye seems tae lawn oan iz feet**.

Lay aff Suspend; expostulate.

Lee To leave; a falsehood.

Leed The metal, lead: **Ma feet's like leed**.

Leedpinsil A lead pencil.

Leer A person who tells lies: **Yurra blirry leer!**

Leez Leaves; leave us/me: **Leez alane** (Leave me alone!).

Len To lend; a loan: **Geez a lenny yer spunks** (Kindly give me a loan of your matches).

Leninlybry A lending library.

Lentil Framework of a door.

Libel Responsible for; apt: **He's libel tae flee aff ra haunle** (He is liable to fly off the handle).

Lick Partake; participate: **He nivver said, 'Collie, wid ye lick?'** (He did not invite me to have a share).

Lifelang During a lifetime.

Like So to speak, used often at the end of a phrase or sentence: **He feenisht up in a coamytoes condeetion, like**.

Likesy People of the kind: **Ah've nae time furra likesy him.**

Lintie A linnet: **There she wiz, singan awaw like a lintie.**

Lip Impudence: **Nane o yer lip, Jimmy!**

Lippie An impudent girl or woman.

Lissless Tired, jaded, without energy.

Lit Permit; leave; let: **Ra trouble wi yew is, ye'll no lit hings alane** (You won't leave things alone).

Loabydoasser A person who sleeps rough in lobbies and closes; often applied to a tout or tip-off man who hangs about premises such as a law court or a newspaper office.

Load Too much to drink.

Loass To lose: **Ye'll no loass much** (It will be no loss).

Loatry A gamble or raffle: **Aw life's a loatry.**

Loowarrum Lukewarm.

Lovely Well done, especially in sport.

Lowdoon Inside information; a revelation about personalities.

Lowss Loose.

Lowze To set free.

Lowzintime End of work.

Luck To look.

Ludger A lodger.

Lugs Ears: **That yin's aw lugs** (That person is always listening/eavesdropping).

Lum A chimney.

Lumber Girl-friend or wife.

M

Mac Mode of address to any man, more cordial than 'Jimmy'.

Mack A maggot.

Maister A boss or a male teacher.

Maitter Matter: **Whitsa maitter?**; **It dizny maitter**.

Mangy Mean.

Manky Unclean.

Maroon Shoothers My round shoulders: a supporter of Heart of Midlothian FC.

Marra The inner substance of a bone; another version of **maitter**: **Whitsa marra wi yew?**

Marrafack As a matter of fact.

Massacred With cosmetics applied to the eyes.

Merch The month of March; to march.

Merchinoarders The sack.

Merkit Market.

Meelimood Afraid to speak one's mind.

Men Repair; heal; the process of healing: **Hoo're ye daein? – Ach, Ah'm oan ra men**.

Mennal Wrong in the head.

Mennin A minnow, usually a 'baggit' one.

Mennit Mended, repaired: **Least said, shinnest mennit**.

Merr Mare; more: **ra merr ra merrier** (the more the merrier).

Merridge A wedding.

Merrit Married.

Merry Marry; Mary.

Midden An untidy place or person; a refuse heap or dump: **at the scaffies' (dustmen's) picnic at Dunoon, Big Wull wiz that owrecome wi the fresh err, they hud tae haud um owre a midden tae revive um**. Chairman of the dustmen's social and dance: **Ah regret Ah huv tae draw thur proceedins tae a**

49

close, as the gentlemen hiz aw tae be in their middens be the moarnin.

Midgie An annoying fly which frequents Rouken Glen and is particularly unkind to kilties.

Mine Care: **Whit'll ye hae? – Ah dinny mine.** Also, remember: **D'ye mine ma face?**

Minereader The wife.

Mines Mine: **Hauns aff! Adze mines.**

Minsh Meat chopped up into very small pieces.

Minsh 'n 'totties Mince and potatoes; the Glasgow coat of arms.

Mirk The dark.

Mirky Overcast, cloudy.

Miscoont A bad enumeration.

Miskerry To go wrong.

Missis Form of address to a lady; the wife.

Mister Form of address to a man.

Moarnin The first drink of the day: **It's a fine moarnin, missis – Ay, but hauf o't's fur anurra wumman.**

Moarn's moarn Tomorrow morning.

Moarra Next day.

Moarrabike A motorcycle.

Moarraboat A speedboat.

Moarracaur A car.

Moarralarry A motor lorry.

Moartal Fatal; drunk.

Moartcherry Place where the dead are kept for identification.

Moass That which a rolling stone does not gather.

Money Many: **Ah huvny saw ye fur money a year**.

Monk An anthropoid ape or a monkey.

Moo The mouth.

Mooch To beg.

Moocher A sponge.

Moose A mouse, hence the Glasgow man's remark on seeing a stuffed moose in the museum: **If that's a moose, Ah wunner whit their rats are like**.

Moosetrap Run-of-the-mill cheese.

Moosybroon A description of hair of indefinite colour.

Mooth Same as **moo**.

Moothfy A mouthful: **Ah'll jiss hae a moothfy; Damn the fears, ye'll jiss get a gless the same as the rest**.

Moothoargan A harmonica.

Moothpiece A shop steward, lawyer or other spokesman.

Muckle Much; large.

Muckmidden A terrible mess: **Ye'll no make a muckmidden o this hoose**.

Mud Ill repute: **Yer name's mud roon here**.

Mug A born loser, at boxing, etc.

Mum Form of address to a lady.

Mun Form of address to a man: **Haud yer hoarses, mun!** (Don't be in quite such a hurry, my dear sir!).

Muncle My uncle.

Murnins Black clothes worn in mourning.

Murnlaw Mother-in-law.

Murra Mother.

Murranfarra Parents.

Murraperil The shiny, variegated inside of an oyster shell.

Muttonfistit Heavy-handed.

Muttonheed A stupid person.

Nae No. See also **borra**.

N

Nab To capture: **Ay, ye aye manage tae nab the biggest daud.**

Nabs Nobility, in the phrase **His Nabs** (His Lordship), applied to many a 'china' with no real claim to rank.

Nae No. See also **borra**.

Nae wey No way, a naturalised 'in-phrase'.

Naitral Natural.

Naitur Nature.

Nakit In the nude. See also **scuddie**.

Nane None, occurring in double negatives: **Ah've no goat nane.**

Naphthy Whisky.

Nark A nagging person; a police informer.

Naw No – in reply to a query.

Neb Nose: **Ye should keep yer neb oot it, but.**

Ned A crook or hooligan.

Neebur A neighbour.

Needle Spite; keen (of a fight or competition where there is an element, not only of rivalry, but of revenge).

Neegur To head a football.

Neep Turnip: **Champit totties and basht neeps** (mashed potatoes and turnips, the usual accompaniment to haggis on ceremonial occasions).

Newfangelt Something new in technique or notions.

Newfarrant The same.

Nick The police cells: **If ye go oan like that, it's the nick ye'll be gettin.**

Nip A half-glass of whisky; 'a wee hauf'; sometimes just a damp glass.

No Not: **no nane** (not any); **no likely** (definitely not).

Noak A clock: **granfarra noak** (a grandfather clock).

Noanstoap An express train or bus.

Node A sharp inclination of the head indicating assent or recognition: **oan the node** (on credit or tick).

Nor Than: **rether yew nor me** (I am glad it is you that is involved and not I).

Nose Crook whose job is to spy out the land for the gang, or 'case the joint'.

Nosebag The dining table: **Yer face is nivver oot ra nosebag.**

Nosedive Dropping to the floor of the ring, pretending to be knocked out: **He waantit me tae dae a nosedive in the saicont roon. He didny ken Ah nivver went intae the saicont roon.** Also known as a **tank joab.**

Note A knot: **He's a right Tewchter: he steers his purritch wi a chanter tae get ra notes.**

Notit Celebrated.

Nut Not (emphatic), often answered by **sut**: **Ah did nut – Ye did sut.**

Nutataw Certainly not.

Nutbroon Brown like a nut: **'Ho, ro, ma nutbroon maiden'.**

Nutter A crazy person: **An utter nutter.**

Nye And me, as in **atween yew nye** (between you and me).

Neep Turnip: **Campit totties and basht neeps** (mashed potatoes and turnips, the usual accompaniment to haggis on ceremonial occasions).

O

Oaf Scots-English for **aff**.

Oaligies The Sciences and Technicalities: **Ah've nae time fur aw thae oaligies**.

Oalivile Oil extracted from the olive; Popeye's girlfriend.

Oamnibus A large volume of stories.

Oan Not off: **oan ra coamitee** (in the favoured inner circle, where the drinks are); **oan an aff** (now and then).

Oancoast A bonus.

Oanty Wise to: **Ah shin goat oanty that wan** (I soon got wise to that two-timer).

Oaperation A surgical treatment, such as getting a joke into a Scotsman's head (according to the Reverend Sidney Smith).

Oapizit Forenent.

Oapryhoose Something they never managed to get in Edinburgh.

Oapt oot Prevent part of your union dues from going to the Labour Party.

Oar To row: **Kin Ah no get oarin ra boat, Paw?**; also **an oarin boat** (a rowing boat).

Oaraitin Making speeches.

Oarder A command.

Oarderly One in attendance to carry out orders.

Oargun A musical instrument.

Oargy A big feed.

Oarickle The way in, or over, some obstacle: **Ah see ye've managed tae work the oarickle**.

Oaritorio A bun-fight with music.

Oaritur A speaker on Glasgow Green.

Oarnery Unassuming: **He wiz only an oarnery warkin chap**.

Oarniment Something fancy or decorative: **Ye're nae oarniment tae Glasga**.

Oasculator A moving staircase in a department store.

Ode Not yielding a whole number when divided by two; peculiar: **D'ye no hink iz a bit ode?** (Do you not think he is a trifle peculiar?).

Odeflah A member of the Oddfellows, or any peculiar male.

Odes A difference: **It dizny mak nae odes** (It's all the same).

Oor Our; hour; **Whan are we gettin oor tea? – In an oor, mebbies.**

Oors Plural of hour; also, belonging to us.

Oorsels Ourselves.

Oot Not in.

Ootcome Result.

Ootcry Protest.

Ootgauns Outlay.

Ootlook Prospect: **There's no much ootlook furra young yins noo.**

Ootnoot Thorough: **Iz an ootnoot blaggird.**

Ootrawey Remote; way out; Excuse me!

Ootrawindae Expelled.

Ootstaunin Conspicuous; remaining.

Ooty Finished: **We're clean ooty crisps.**

Open-haunit Generous.

Open-hertit Sincere.

Openin-time What the flahs are waiting for.

Open-mooed Astonished.

Open-myndit Not caring who beats the Rangers (or the Celtic, according to one's personal stance).

Owl Old: **ma owl man** (my father).

Owrack To overact.

Owre Over; above; finished: **It's aw owre an din wi**; too much, in excess: **That's five pee owre**; excessively: **Ye're owre pleased wi yersell, ma man.**

P

Paaltry Trivial: **It wiz that paaltry ye should nivver huv took it.**

Packhoarse Horse used to carry packs: **The wife aye hiz me loadit up like a packhoarse.**

Paddy Temper: **Ye dinny need tae get yer paddy up at me.**

Paddytrain Train to Glasgow from the boat crossing from Ireland.

Padjin A picturesque procession.

Pailfy The fill of a pail: **He's drank a pailfy since he cam in.**

Painfy Causing pain: **It's no that it's serr: it's painfy forbye.**

Pammy The old-fashioned punishment of schoolchildren inflicted on the palm with a leather strap.

Pant A comical situation (abbreviated from the next entry): **Laugh? It wiz a rale pant.**

Pantymine The regular Christmas entertainment of old Glaswegians: **Ah'll nivver forget Doris Droy in the aul Queen's Pantymine, or George West at the Princess.**

Paradise Celtic's football ground.

Parliment The loo.

Parlirabat Talk a foreign language.

Parry A political group, such as **ra Labour Parry.**

Parryfinile Paraffin.

Partickler Choosy: **Whit'll ye hae? – Ah'm no partickler.**

Pastaff Cleared: **Ah hud serr teeth but it's pastaff.**

Pastmaister An expert: **That wan's a pastmaister at bummin a drink.**

Pastoot Succumbed: **Mebbie ye nivver noticed but yer china's pastoot.**

Pastowre Overlooked, ignored: **Ah wiz efter a joab as a news announcer oan the BBC, but Ah wiz pastowre.**

Pat Word-perfect: **Whan ye tell a lee, ye've goat tae huv it aff pat.**

Pate Peter.

Patter Banter; swank: **Iz no hauf pittin oan the patter; Ay, his patter stinks.**

Pauchle A bundle; a rake-off.

Paw Affectionate name for father.

Pawky Droll: **Iz awfy pawky, inty?** (He is very droll, isn't he?).

Pawn A cloth hung round the edge of a bed.

Pawnmaw One's parents: **Pawnmaw an ra wains** (the family).

Pech To puff and pant.

Peck A lot: **Ye'll eat a peck o dirt afore ye dee.**

Peeky Ill-looking: **Ma man's kinny peeky ranoo, well.**

Peelaff Do a striptease.

Peelywally Delicate.

Peen Pin; **peens an needles** (prickly sensation when circulation is restored).

Peen doon Bind to a contract.

Peeny A pinafore; also the stomach: **Ah've a pain in ma peeny, but.**

Peety A pity. Used sarcastically in **It's a peety furrum**.

Peg oot Die.

Pelmet A miniskirt.

Pen An archway leading to an alley: **Jiss go through at pen owre err, see?**

Pent Paint.

People Us: **We arra people**.

Perch In the expression, **Iz fell aff iz perch** (He has dropped off to sleep).

Perish An old word for social security: **That wan's been oana perish since ivver Ah've kent um**.

Perishin Cold: **Whit's it like oot? – Perishin**; also sometimes used as a mild adjective or adverb, in mixed company.

Perisht Feeling the cold: **Ah dinny ken aboot yew, but Ah'm perisht**.

Perkin A ginger biscuit.

Perky In good fettle.

Perm Hit over the head: **Try that yince merr an Ah'll perm ye**.

Perner Partner.

Perpendickler Bolt upright: **He wiz frichtit perpendickler**.

Perr Pear; pare; poor; pair: **a rerr perr** (a good pair).

Perra A pair of: **Ma wain could dae wi a new perra shin** (My child is in need of a new pair of shoes).

Perrs hoose The poorhouse, a memory of the past: **That wife o mine, she'll hae me in the perrs hoose**.

Persley A green herb used in cooking.

Pert Portion; piece; role in a play; part: **He taen it in guid pert**, but: **Whan Ah wiz a wee lassie, Ah hud a starrin pert in the Sunny Skill kinnerspiel**; to separate: **Ra besty freens muss pert, but**.

Pertial Biased in favour: **Ah wiz nivver awrat pertial tae ra telly**.

Pertin Separation: **It wizny whit ye'd caw a serr pertin fae ma murnlaw**.

Pertly Not entirely.

Perty A celebration.

Peter oot To go out ignominiously.

Pewmoany Pneumonia.

Pey Wages.

Pey aff To render redundant.

Phase oot Gradually do without.

Photy Portrait.

Photygenic Goodlooking: **See at photygenic chat owre err!**

Photyphoby Morbid hatred of being photographed, especially by the police.

Photystat A copy.

Phut Collapsed: **It wiz like a daith in the hoose whan wur telly went phut.**

Physic Medicine such as **casterile, gnat, an ippycakeyannie wine, gnat.**

Picker A connoisseur, especially of the opposite sex: **Ye're a guid picker, but.**

Picnic A good time: **It's nae picnic, Ah kin tell ye.**

Picterhoose A cinema.

Picters The movies; illustrations: **It's no muchy a book – nae picters.**

Pie A walkover: **It wiz a right piece o pie.**

Piece A sandwich taken to work or thrown to a child from a tenement window.

Piece ragirra To fit details together into a whole.

Pie 'n' peez A favourite dish from the old-time Tallyshoaps.

Pierrots Seaside entertainers: **See oapry? Ah'd rether go tae the pierrots.**

Pigeon-chistit With an exaggerated bosom.

Pigheedit Obstinately following the wrong football club.

Pigheeditness Refusal to see one's point of view.

Pile Fortune: **Zat yew, pooin oot, efter ye've made yer pile?**

Pilfer Purpose of a prescription from the doctor: **Whitzat pilfer?**

Pirn A bobbin used in spinning and weaving.

Pit To place: **Pit a boab oan it fur me, well!**

Pitchentoass A game of quoits with coins.

Pitchers A variant of **picters** (the movies).

Pitchfoark To thrust someone into a situation against his will.

Pitten Put (past participle): **Anurra crack like that an yew'll get pitten oot.**

Pizzicoalijy The science of reading the mind; a famous racehorse.

Plantit Of stolen property, concealed to incriminate an innocent party.

Platefy The fill of a plate; an embarrassment: **Dinny expeck me tae haunle it: Ah've a platefy tae be gaun oan wi.**

Plates Feet: **Shift yer plates, Jimmy!** (Kindly remove your feet, dear sir).

Play-ackin Pretending.

Play-aff To begin a game; to exploit one against another, 'divide and conquer': **She's jiss playin at flah aff agane Cherlie.**

Playgrun Piece of ground beside school, for recreation.

Play oan Resume the game; to deceive: **She's jiss playin oan ye.**

Plenny Sufficient.

Plenny bags More than sufficient.

Ploader A steady worker.

Ploat To scald – for instance, a chicken before plucking.

Ploatit Scalded.

Plooky Pimply-faced.

Plumduff Christmas pudding.

Plumpudden Variant of the aforegoing.

Plunk To put down heavily: **Dinny go plunkin yer dough oan that aul kert-hoarse.**

Plywid A wood made of several layers.

Poalicies The back green: **Ah'm jiss haein a dauner roon ra poalicies.**

Poalish From Poland or thereabout; stuff for cleaning shoes; the Polish language; style: **At flah's goat poalish.**

Poalish aff Devour; defeat; murder.

Poalitician A character seen around only at election-time.

Poalitics Arguments about Celtic and Rangers.

Poassible Capable of occurring.

Poasskerd A card designed for posting.

Poassman A letter carrier.

Poat A receptacle; a tummy, hence **big poat** (an eminent citizen); **jack poat** (the big win in a competition).

Poat-hole A hole in the road.

Poatit heed Dead: **Ay, ma femly'll appreeshit me whan Ah'm poatit heed.**

Poat-shoat A random volley.

Poet Someone who inadvertently breaks into rhyme: **Hae, yew're a poet an ye don't know it.**

Poke A sack; a paper or plastic bag.

Poke aboot Meddle; try to uncover some sinister facts.

Poky Jail; also, a bag of, as in **a poky chips.**

Poky hat An ice-cream cornet; a clown's or pierrot's hat.

Polis The law; **lassie polis** (a policewoman).

Poliscaur Vehicle used by police.

Poliscoort Court presided over by a magistrate.

Polisman A limb of the law.

Pome A rhymed address to a girl friend; a greeting or *in memoriam* in verse.

Pon A small lake: **juck pon** (a pool frequented by ducks).

Poo To pull: **Poo yersell ragirra, mac!** (Pull yourself together, my friend!); a pulling motion: **Gie't a sherp poo, Jimmy!**; **Poo, paw, poo!** (the Chinese sound of a Glasgow boy telling his father what to do in an oarin boat).

Poo aff To bring a project to a successful conclusion.

Poodle A small pool of water caused by rain, whence the Glasgow comic's chestnut: **It's rainin cats an dugs: Ah stepped oan a poodle.**

Poo doon To humble.

Pool A pub game; a football lottery; a bunch of typists.

Poor To pour; power.

Poorfy Powerful.

Poorie A teapot.

Pooroot A scattering of largesse at a wedding.

Poothroo An appliance for cleaning the barrel of a rifle.

Pope Ginger beer.

Popecoarn Popcorn.

Popelar Well-liked; one of three kinds of trees recognised by army sergeants for range-finding, the other two being 'fir trees' and 'bushy-topped trees'.

Porkypine An animal with protective quills.

Portugee A native of Portugal, (plural, **Porkanbeans**).

Precinx Area surrounding a building.

Preen Variant of **peen**, found in phrases such as **hat preen**, **herr preen**, **safety preen** and **claes preen**.

Preperr Make ready; anticipate, as in the Scout motto, **Be Preperred**.

Prig A thief.

Prirority A course of action foremost for action: **A better deal furra warkers is ra first prirority**.

Proablem Something awaiting solution: **Adze yewr proablem, Jimmy**.

Proacrastinater A con-man.

Proagnoasticater Another con-man, or perhaps the same one.

Proaliterriat Us.

Proamnent Outstanding; distinguished; large; **a proamnent neb** (a Roman nose).

Proapaganna Lies printed in Edinburgh about Glasgow.

Proavist The civic head, sometimes dignified as '**ra Lore Proavist**'.

Prood Possessed of pride; **Ye done us prood, son**.

Pru An insurance company or its representative: **Here ra Pru; ur ye in?**

Puck To punish at school with the tawse.

Pudden A dumpling; a haggis; a 'mealie pudden'; a footballer who foozles a kick.

Pudden supper Chips with haggis or 'mealie pudden'.

Pug A boxer, especially one with the earmarks.

Puggelt Drunk.

Puggie A monkey; bad temper: **Noo dinny yew be gettin ma puggie up**.

Puggienuts Peanuts.

Pump To extract information: **Ye kin pump a well, Jimmy, but ye canny pump me**.

Punna lynx A pound of sausages.

Punters Us.

Putrit Common criticism of a game or show which has not come up to expectations. **Whid-ye hink o't? – Putrit**.

Q

Quack One's doctor.

Quawnity Amount: **That wan'll drink ony given quawnity.**

Quawrra A fourth part.

Quawrramaister Officer attending to supplies; petty officer at sea.

Quawrramiler Runner specialising in the quarter mile.

Quids in Highly successful; sitting pretty.

Quippy Repartee.

Quirk A catch or let-down: **Ah shouldy kent they wur a quirk in it.**

Quits. Revenge; evening up: **Ah'll be quits wi um afore Ah'm feenisht.**

Quod The Bar L.

Quorum A bunch of cronies at a bar, sufficiently large to accommodate a 'jyner'.

Rappelle Celebrated Glasgow beginning of a song: **'Rappelle moon wiz shinin. . .'**

R

Ra The definite article, in many combinations.

Rab Haw The legendary Glasgow glutton who, when asked if he'd have his meal *à la carte*, replied: **Och, naw, Ah'll jiss hae a barraload tae be gaun oan wi.**

Rabid Description of one who disagrees with one.

Raggit In rags.

Raggit skill School to which poor children, at one time, were sent; now used in the expression: **Whit raggit skill wiz it yew went tae?**

Rainfaw Precipitation of rain.

Rake-aff Protection money; commission.

Rale Genuine.

Rammy An uproar, often on a 'sterrheed'.

Ramstam Moving heavily and uncouthly: **He's a ramstam, big-fittit juck, that wan.**

Ramstoory Rash, reckless.

Ran Past tense of 'run', frequently used as past participle, as in **Ah've went an ran ooty chynge, china.**

Rang Rung: **Ye've nivver rang ra bell, Jimmy.**

Rank bad yin An out-and-out rascal.

Rap The blame: **Ah've hud tae take ra rap furraw ra resty yiz** (I have had to accept the blame on behalf of all of you).

Rappelle Celebrated Glasgow beginning of a song: **'Rappelle moon wiz shinin. . .'**

Rasp Rude noise made anciently at the Trongate Panopticon and later at various variety halls, in criticism.

Rat A traitor; to betray.

Rats A hangover. **Dinny speak tae um, iz inna rats ziss moarnin.**

Rattelt Annoyed, disconcerted.

Ratty Angry.

Rebile Boil over again.

Red To tidy: **Red up this room noo, Jinty!**; rid: **We'll jiss hae tae get red o um.**

Redunnancy The golden handshake.

Reel To go in circles.

Reperr Restore: **This hoose is needin reperred.**

Respeck To heed, appreciate: **They've nae respeck fur us aul yins.**

Ressarum The remainder.

Resscure A long lie.

Ressless Fidgeting.

Restrickit Confined.

Rether Sooner, rather.

Rhubart Rhubarb.

Rid Red.

Rid-haunit Red-handed.

Ridheedit Red-headed; reckless: **He went at it ridheedit.**

Rid injin A boy with a Mohican haircut.

Rift To belch.

Rine The outer coat of cheese or bacon; a rein.

Rise Ridicule: **She's jiss takin a rise oot ye.**

Rode Ridden: **This hoarse hiz nivver been rode be this joackey afore.**

Romannic Amorous.

Roon Round.

Roonaboot In the vicinity; approximately; indirect: **Yoan wiz a gey roonaboot wey tae come here.**

Roonaff Conclude; put the finishing touches to.

Roonroabin A petition to the management with signatures in a ring. As with the computer, 'naebody gets the blame'.

Roonshoothert Traditional condition of an Edinburgh man who persists in supporting Heart of Midlothian FC (Maroon Shoothers).

Roon trip Return journey.

Roonup Collect: **Roonup ra boays!** (Collect the gang!).

Roosty Covered with rust.

Rooze To arouse; to make bad-tempered: **Noo dinny yew rooze me, or ah'll soart ye!**

Ropy Rough, of football or a show.

Rose Risen: **Ye should uv rose hauf an oor ago.**

Row To roll.

Rowan Rolling: **Maw, kin we get rowan wur Easter eggs?**; also, a mountain-ash.

Rub aff To adhere from contact: **Ah like hingan aboot millionerrs – ye nivver ken, it might rub aff oan ye.**

Rubbish A person or persons for whom one has contempt: **Ah widny assoashet wi um: iz rubbish.**

Rub doon To administer an invigorating towelling or massage.

Rummle To see through a swindle or attempt at deception: **Ah wiz owre fly furrum: Ah rummelt um right away.**

Run doon To denigrate, usually on the 'sterrheed'.

Run efter To chase; to lavish attention on.

Runnan coamintry A football report from the ground; the chattering of a talkative spectator or bystander: **Staun aside that wan, an ye'll be sherry a runnan coamintry.**

Runooty Exhaust: **Awra coamics is beginnan tae runooty ideas.**

Runowre Overflow; knock down by vehicle.

Rush To hustle; to be impatient with: **Dinny rush me! Thur plenny time.** Also a rash on the skin: **The wain's went an cam oot in a rush.**

S

Sable He is capable: **Sable fur ony-hing.**

Sackbut Dismissal, notwithstanding: **Ye'll get the sackbut.**

Sackfy The fill of a sack.

Saft Soft; wet; or foolish person; hence **safty.**

Saluki A striking resemblance: **Saluki iz farra aboorrum** (There is a look of his father about him).

Sam Broon An officer's belt.

Sang Song; sung: **If iz sang that sang wance iz sang it a thoosan times.**

Sangimoanious Hypocritical.

Sannie Claus Father Christmas: **If yewze wains dinny behave yersell Sannie Claus'll no come doon that lum.**

Sannies Rubber and canvas shoes.

Sannitches Sandwiches.

Sannitry A health inspector: **Ah'll get ra sannitry tae yiz.**

Sark Shirt: **See that wannacloak gun through in Embruh? Ah jump oot ma sark ivvery time Ah hear it.**

Saun Sand: **Lift that wain, its dowp's choakit wi saun! Dippit inna watter, well!**

Saunbag Bag filled with sand; to smite someone with such a weapon; also used, more congenially, in the phrase, **laffin saunbags** (well off).

Saunboax Box filled with sand or grit for treatment of icy roads.

Saunflee A sandhopper insect.

Saun gless An egg-timer.

Saunpaper Gritty paper for smoothing; to smoothe thus.

Saunstane Quarried building material.

Sauny Alexander.

Sausitches Sausages: **Sausitches izza boays!**

Saut Salt: **That lad's needan saut pitten oan iz tail.**

Sautcellar Holder for table salt.

Sautmarket A Glasgow thoroughfare.

Sautwatter The sea.

Sauty Flavour with salt.

Sauty totties Sauté potatoes.

Savvy Commonsense; comprehension; to understand: **Iz goat nae savvy, he jiss dizny savvy – savvy?**

Saw Seen: **Ah've nivver saw sich a kerry-oan afore!**

Scabbit In poor condition.

Scad To scald.

Scaddit Of skin, inflamed by rubbing in frosty conditions.

Scale Of a school, to dismiss: **The skill's scalin.**

Scannelmunger The wife next door.

Scanny Insufficient: **They gie ye gey scanny meezher.**

Scliff Soft-shoe dance.

Scoaff Food: **Whit's ra scoaff like in Eye-beeza?**

Scoat A native of Scoatlan.

Scoatch Scottish.

Scoatchman A Scotsman.

Scoatchwumman A Scotswoman.

Scoatlan Scotland.

Scoonrel A bad character.

Scoor To scour.

Scoorer A cloth for scouring.

Scooroot A laxative.

Scootoot To ferret out.

Scooty Small; inadequate: **Ah've oanly a scooty wee pension, so Ah huv.**

Scran Food: **See me? Ah kin aye go ma scran.**

Scrap A fight or a boxing match.

Scrapper A pugilist.

Scratchy A tramp.

Scrubber A despicable person.

Scruff Riff-raff; 'students gnat'.

Scud State of nature, used in the expression **in ra scud**.

Scuddie Naked; a nude: **Hae, here some scuddies! – Are they men or weemen? – Ah'm damned if Ah ken, they've nae claes oan!**

Seafern Following the sea: **Ye kin easy tell iz a seafern man.**

Seagaun Ocean-bound.

Seaseek Upset by the rocking of the boat.

Sect Given the heave.

Sectry A secretary.

See A word much used in Glasgow to introduce a subject of conversation: **See thae MPs? They're rubbish; See ma murra? She widny truss me as faur as she could throw me.**

See aboot To attend to.

See aff Bid farewell to.

Seek Sick: **awfy seek** (terribly sick).

Seekint Put off.

Seeknin Off-putting: **Ay, it's seeknin, intit?**

Seekscunnert Absolutely disgusted.

See oot Outlive: **The owl wan'll see me oot yet, but.**

Seize Let me have: **Seize owre at screwdriver.**

Seleck Very posh.

Sell Self: **He done it aw iz sell.**

Senninst Sentenced.

Sennrygo Guard duty.

Septical Disbelieving.

Serr Sore: **Sawfy serr** (It's very sore).

Serr een Sore eyes: **a sicht for serr een** (a pleasant surprise).

Serrjint Sergeant: **Tell that man to get down off the skyline! – Adze no a man, sir, adze oor serrjint.**

Set tae A fight.

Shaddyboaxin Make-believe: **See thae MPs? They're jiss shaddyboaxin.**

Shakes Status: **Iz nae great shakes, but.**

Shanks' powny By foot: **See thae Glasga buses? Ah'd rether go Shanks' powny.**

Shannygaff Beer and aerated water mixed.

Shattert Astounded, flabbergasted.

Shave A slice: **A shave aff a cut loaf's nivver missed.**

Shawlie A woman wearing a shawl in the earlier part of the century.

Sheek A lady-killer, or one who thinks he is.

Sheekles Money.

Sheeps-heed The head of a sheep and the broth made from it.

Sheers Scissors.

Shellackin A beating.

Sherr Sure.

Sherrickin A scolding and showing-up before one's chinas.

Shin Shoes; soon.

Shirty Angry.

Shoag A nudge; to shake.

Shoak Something which astonishes.

Shoap Shop; to give away to the police: **It wiz his ain farra at shoapt um.**

Shoartdowp A short person.

Shoarts Short trousers.

Shoart-tempert Easy to annoy.

Shoart-winnit Breathless.

Shoat A shot; rid: **He wiz aff like a shoat; Ah shin goat shoaty um.**

Shoo To sew.

Shoogyshoo To swing, especially a baby.

Shoother Shoulder. Sometimes **shoora.**

Shove aff Get out of my sight.

Shuch A ditch; muck.

Shuffle A shovel.

Shug Hugh.

Shuge Huge.

Shuman Human, as in **shuman bean.**

Shumid Humid.

Shut Drunk. Thus, **hauf shut** means half drunk.

Sich Such, sometimes **sich 'n.**

Sidieweys Sideways; laterally.

Siller Money: **Ah've ran ooty siller, but.**

Singsang An impromptu concert; also, the lilt of Edinburgh speech, as distinct from that of Glasgow: **See thae Embruh folk? Ye kin aye tell them be their singsang.**

Sinner A fellow: **It wizny me, it mussuv been some urra sinner.**

Sizer Something big.

Skart Scratch: **Dinny skart yer heed, son, ye'll get skelfs.**

Skelf A splinter, especially if lodged in the finger.

Skelly Squint-eyed.

Sketch Take a good look at: **Sketch that funny-luckan guy.**

Skew-whiff Squint.

Skids A treacherous slide: **Ah'll shin pit ra skids unner um.**

Skill School.

Skillbooks School literature.

Skill chum Schoolmate.

Skillmaister A male teacher.

Skillteacher Usually a woman teacher.

Skilly Slate-pencil, a memory of the past.

Skin Rake-off.

Skirl Squeal. Never to be applied to the bagpipes in front of the cognoscenti.

Skive To dodge work; to smoke in the loo.

Skiver An habitual workshy.

Sky diver The same.

Slaister To work sloppily and untidily; one who does this.

Slates Out of reach: **Ra baw's oan ra slates** (The game is up).

Slaver A person who talks rubbish.

Slide Deterioration, especially of a boxer: **He's oan ra slide** (He is losing his silk).

Slitter An untidy worker.

Slog To fight in a round-arm fashion.

Slogger A round-arm, wild, unscientific boxer.

75

Slug To knock out, with a cosh, for instance.

Smaw Little.

Snag Stickjaw toffee.

Snaw Snow.

Sneck Latch.

Soady waste A wasteland on the bank of the Clyde near Rutherglen.

Soarra Sorrow.

Soarry Excuse me!

Soart To sort out; to finish: **Pipe doon or Ah'll soart ye!**

Soarty Rather: **Ah thoat he wiz a soarty funny guy.**

Soo Female pig.

Soom To swim.

Soon Sound: **It dizny soon aw that great tae me.**

Soonoot To find out what people are thinking.

Soop To sweep: **Soop ra flerr, owre err!** (Sweep the floor over there).

Soor Sour.

Soorface A grouser.

Sooth The South.

Sparra Small finch-like bird, *Passer domesticus*.

Sparralan A slum.

Specky doadle A person who wears glasses.

Spen To spend.

Spinfy A spoonful; a small quantity: **Whit'll ye hae? – Jist a spinfy.**

Spoke Spoken.

Spoot To gush; a tap: **Ra tea's owre weak tae come oot ra spoot.**

Sproot A young shoot; to shoot up, grow: **Ye're sprootan a berd areddies** (You're growing a beard already); Boy Scout (facetious); leafy vegetable: **Brussels sproots.**

Spunk A match: **a boaxy spunks** (a box of matches); **Seeza spunk, mac!** (Please give me a match, sir).

Sp'yug Same as **sparra.**

Squawker One who 'clypes' to ra polis.

Squeejee Squint: **Jings, yer cherr's aw squeejee.**

Squerr Square; to bribe someone; level: **Ziss oana squerr?** (Is this on the level?); **aw squerr** (level scores); even: **Ah'll get squerr wi um yit, but.**

Squerrheed A Teuton.

Squerrtaed Having square toes.

Stank A drain, especially at the end of a gutter.

Starknaikit In the nude.

Starturn Any comic, sometimes used sarcastically: **Ye're a starturn right enough, but.**

Staun To stand; a stand: **Ye've goat tae take a staun.**

Staunup Contend for rights; standing up: **staunup coamic** (comedian who stands at the microphone with patter and 'nae ack' – no act); **a staunup fight.**

Stave To dislocate or stub – a finger or toe, for instance **A gaun fit's aye gettin, though it be but a staved tae.**

Steer To stir: **Is there nae sugar in this tea? – There is if ye steer it.**

Stepbrurra Stepbrother. By analogy, **stepfarra, stepmurra**, etc.

Stern Staring: **Whit-ye stern at, Jimmy?**

Sterr Stair; to stare.

Sterrheed The top of a staircase: **Sterrheed stushie** (an altercation in a tenement).

Stewart A steward.

Stick Criticism: **Ah'm gettin plenny stick, but.**

Stiffner A punter whose bet stops a horse from winning.

Stirling See **stuckie**.

Stoack A wooden post.

Stoackstill Motionless.

Stoap To cease: **Stoap muckan aboot!**

Stoapper The lid of a bottle: **Ah've saw ra day Ah could caw croon stoappers aff wi ma teeth.**

Stoarrum A turbulence.

Stookie A tailor's dummy; a useless person.

Stookiedoll A stuffed representation of a face at which competitors shied wooden balls at the shows.

Story A rumour, disbelieved: **Adze jist a story, but.**

Strag An errand.

Stramash A riot.

Strang Virile: **Iz no a verra strang flah** (He is not a very strong chap).

Stuckie A starling, also known as a **stirling.**

Stuffin Infernal internals: **Ah'll caw ra stuffin ooty ye.**

Stummel To find something out by accident: **Ah've jiss stummelt oan a funny hing.**

Stushie An altercation. See **sterrheed.**

Suboarnit Lower in rank.

Swam Swum.

Swarrum A crowd, of bees, flies, people, gnat.

Sweer To swear: **Ye dinny need tae sweer, but**; reluctant: **He wiz gey sweer tae get oan wi't.**

Sweet Perspiration: **Whit wi ra heat'n ra sweet'n ra smell urra beer. . .**

Sweethert Mode of address by bus-driver to lady passenger.

Sweety A confection; a girl-friend.

Swey To move unsteadily; to influence: **Naebdy could swey rum oan Glasga Green like Jimmy Maxton, but.**

Swore Sworn: **Ah could uv swore it wiz yew.**

T

Tack Discretion: **Iz jiss goat nae tack, that wan.**

Tackless Devoid of discretion.

Taen Taken; took: **He taen wan luck at me an beat it.**

Tally An Italian.

Tallyshoap An icecream or fish-and-chip shop run by someone of Italian descent.

Tannalize Annoy; torment.

Tap To scrounge; the act of begging: **Iz aye oan ra tap.**

Tappietoorie Tassel on the top of a Scotch bonnet.

Tapsalteerie Upside-down.

Tararra A tiara; a loose woman.

Tart A young woman, not necessarily of easy virtue; a sweetheart.

Tawpie A rather stupid girl.

Tawse The leather strap with which Scottish schoolchildren were traditionally punished, on the palm only.

Tealeaf A thief.

Teaspinfy The fill of a teaspoon.

Teer To tear. Also, **terr**.

Teeran Violent; reckless: **Ye dinny need tae be in sich a teeran hurry, ye've jiss goat here.**

Temp To tempt.

Tempan Appealing; succulent. **Could ye no geeze sumpin merr tempan?**

Tempit Influenced by the Devil.

Tempitcher Condition of heat or cold.

Ten To look after.

Tennerhertit Compassionate.

Terr To tear; a good time or a good laugh: **a rerr terr at ra Ferr** (a good time enjoyed at the Glasgow Fair).

Terra To tether: **Ah'm jiss aboot at ra enny ma terra.**

Terriblawful The news; the football results; a newsboy's cry: **Full results urra terriblawful.**

Tewchter A Highlander. See **Heelanman.**

Theeayrra A theatre.

Thickheed A stupid person.

Thickskint Not easily impressed or moved.

Thingme Someone whose name one does not recall: **If ye want me, Thingme, ring me!**

Thingmeboab Some object one has lost the name for.

Thingmejig The same.

Thinskint Over-sensitive: **Ye're owre thinskint, but.**

Thir These.

Thoan Yon.

Thoom The thumb: **Ah've went an goat a skelf in ma thoom** (I have gone and suffered a splinter in my thumb).

Thoozan A thousand: **If Ah've tellt ye wance Ah've telt ye a thoozan times.**

Thoozant The thousandth: **Furra thoozant time, belt up, will ye?**

Thrapple The throat; to strangle: **Ah'll thrapple ye.**

Threed Thread.

Threedberr Badly worn.

Throve Thriven: **He seems tae huv throve on it, but.**

Thunner Thunder.

Thunnerplump Heavy rain accompanying thunder.

Ticket An odd-looking person: **Thoan's an awfy-luckan ticket.**

Ticktack Not only the bookies' sign language but any 'bush telegraph', 'grapevine', 'scuttlebutt' or inside information: **Ye mighta gien me ra ticktack, but.**

Tig Tag, in the children's touch game: **Tig yew're het an Ah'm no playin** (That's enough of that!).

Tiler A person who mends or makes clothes.

Tim Empty. Hence, **timheedit** ignorant.

Timeboax Office where working time is checked.

Timekerrd A card recording working time.

Timmer Wood.

Timmerfit A person with a wooden leg.

Timmeryerd A yard where timber is stored.

Tip A refuse dump.

Tipkert A cart made so as to be tipped.

Tiptae To walk on the tips of the toes: **Ye'll need tae tiptae in.**

Tiptoap First-rate.

Tirl To turn; to twirl; to ring a bell: **Ah'll tirl yer lug tae ye** (I will ring your ear).

Toaper A first-rate person; one who gives lavish tips.

Toapical Of current interest.

Toarnface A persistent grouser.

Toff A well-dressed stranger to the district, especially with a Southern English accent.

Tom Jewellery, from the rhyming slang, 'tomfoolery'.

Toon The town.

Toonheed Townhead.

Toor A tower; high-rise flats.

Toorie Topknot on a bonnet.

Tore Torn: **Ach ye've went an tore it noo.**

Torydore A bullfighter.

Tossle A tassel.

Totie Very small, sometimes **totie-wee.**

Tottie A potato; constituent element of such delicacies as **totties 'n' herrin** and **minsh 'n' totties.**

Tow String; rope.

Track A religious pamphlet.

Trainile Train oil, alleged to be used on some lads' hair. Also used in the phrase: **Sleepan yer brains tae trainile.**

Traivler A traveller, commercial or otherwise.

Trams Feet: **D'ye mine gettin' yer trams ootra road, Jimmy?**

Trap Mouth: **Adze whit wey they caw rum Trappist monks: they hae tae keep their traps shut.**

Trauchle Hard, troublesome work.

Treckle Treacle.

Trecklescoan Treacle scone.

Treed Tread.

Treezhur Treasure.

Troat Trot.

Troch A horse trough.

Troops The lads: **kiddnatroops** (blinding people with science).

Troot Trout.

Troozers Trousers.

Truck Dealings: **Ah widny hae nae truck wirra likesy him.**

Trumfs Trumps at cards.

Try-oan An attempt to deceive.

Try-oot A rehearsal.

Tummle To fall over; to grasp a meaning: **Ah dinny hink ye tummle, mac.**

Tummledoon Dilapidated.

Tummler A beer glass.

Turn doon Reject: **Ye've went an turnt doon yer big chance.**

Twang The funny way they speak in Edinburgh or Aberdeen – or America!

Twaw Two: **Oot, baith ra twaw o yiz!**

Twicer A base deceiver.

Twiss The bend: **Iz roon ra twiss, that wan.**

U

Ulster Ulcer.

Umberella A gamp. See also **Heelanman**.

Unanimous Unsigned.

Unberrable Intolerable.

Uncoark To remove a stopper or stoppage from anywhere.

Unctioneer An auctioneer.

Unction sale Sale by auction.

Undae To cancel out what has been achieved: **Ye'll jiss undae awra guid wark ye've did.**

Undefennit Undefended.

Undone Undid.

Unjyne To separate.

Unkemp Untidy.

Unkent Unknown.

Unlowze Untie.

Unmerrit Single.

Unmethoadicul Lacking in method.

Unner Below.

Unnerclaes Underwear.

Unnercut Sell at a lower price.

Unnerfit Beneath the feet.

Unnergrun The Glasgow Subway.

Unnerstaun To comprehend.

Unnertaker A mortician: **Ye luck as if ye're ready furra unnertaker, mac.**

Unpeyed Unpaid: **Bein a hoosewife is jiss unpeyed labour.**

Unpoaplar In the bad books: **Ah'm unpoaplar wirra wife ra noo.**

Unraivelt Disentangled.

Unrowe To unroll.

Unsocial oors The late shift.

Untruthfy Dishonest.

Unweel Suffering from ill health.

Upsandoons Vicissitudes.

Upshoat The eventual result.

Upside doon Inverted.

Upstert An impudent Johnny-come-lately.

Uptak Perception: **Iz no verra gleg in the uptak**.

Upty Planning something; capable of; understanding: **Whit ye upty? Ye're upty nae guid; Iz no upty it**.

Up wi The matter with: **Whit's up wi ye?** Also, finished: **It's aw up wi um noo**.

Ur Her; are.

Ursell Herself; by herself (alone): **Ma Maw's in ursell** (My mother is in the house by herself).

V

Vannalism Wanton destruction.

Vawz A vase.

Vejtible A friend who won't join the party.

Venter Venture.

Venue The pub.

Venus The barmaid: **Ye mean she's no goat nae errums?**

Verdick Any decision: **Whidza verdick, well?**

Verra Very.

Versytile Clever and entertaining.

Vice Voice.

Vilence Use of force.

Vilent Obstreperous.

Vinnicaitit Justified by events.

Virl A ferrule; a tip on the end of a walking stick.

Voilin A fiddle.

Voilits Nice flowers.

Vultcher An addict: **a vultcher fur cultcher; a vultcher fur punishment.**

W

Waarum Not cold.

Waggitywaw A pendulum clock.

Wagglarakilt The characteristic Scottish soldier's gait.

Walkoot Industrial action; a romantic convoy.

Walkowre An easy victory.

Wallies Dentures.

Wally Ceramic, as in 'wally close' (tiled entry).

Waltz it To win easily.

Wame Stomach: **Iz goat wanny thae beerdrinker's wames.**

Wan Won; one. Same as **yin.**

Wance Once. Same as **yince.**

Wannacloak One o'clock.

Warst The worst; sometimes, worse: **If ye stert some-hing wi me, ye'll get the warst o't.**

Wash-hoose Place for washing; **ra wash-hoose key** (an object of dispute in old tenement days).

Washoot Failure; disappointment.

Wat Wet (adjective).

Watchdug A dog which is good for domestic security; a handy, vigilant neighbour.

Watter The Clyde Estuary. See also **doonrawatter.**

Waur Worse: **nane the waur** (none the worse).

Waw A wall: **Iz hud me climman up ra waw.**

Wee Small; a short while: **Hud yer wheesht a wee!** (Be silent for a moment!).

Weel In good health: **Ah'm no verra weel, well.**

Weemin Plural of **wumman.**

Weers Ours: **It's wan o weers.**

Weet The wet: **Come in ootra weet.**

Well In that case; so; but in Glasgow often heard at the end instead of the beginning of the sentence: **Ye better go hame, well.**

Whit fur? Why?: **Whit fur no?** (Why not?).

Whit wey? How? Why?; Wee MacGreegor's constant query: **Whit wey, Maw?**

Wid Wood; would.

Widden Wooden; **widdenheed** (a fool); **widden leg** (an artificial leg).

Widdy A widow.

Widny Would not.

Win The wind; flatulence: **Ah'm awfy borrad wirra win.**

Winny Will not; windy.

Wirny Were not.

Wirra Accompanying: **oot wirra boays.**

Wiz Was; were: **We wiz robbed.**

Wizny Was not; were not.

Wore Worn: **Ah'm aw wore oot.**

Wrang Wrong.

Wrote Written.

Wumman A woman: **an owl wumman** (an old woman); **a dressed wumman** (a lady). Plural: **weemin.**

Wunner Wonder: **Ay, nae wunner** (Yes, no wonder).

Wunnerfy Miraculous.

Wur Our.

Wurrit Troubled.

Wurrsit Worsted.

Wurruld World.

Wurrum A worm.

X

X-ray A special late edition of a newspaper.

Y

Yaat A yacht: **Yaffa yaat? Whit yaat yaffa?** (Are you from some yacht? What yacht are you from? Question traditionally asked of someone wearing a yachting cap).

Yabble To talk too much.

Yaw You all; all of you: **Ah didny expeck yaw at wance.**

Yellabelly A dark-complexioned person.

Yella yite The yellowhammer bird *(Emberiza citrinella)*; also, anyone wearing something yellow; a traffic warden, because of the yellow tabs.

Yerd A yard.

Yew You (singular, emphatic).

Yin One: Are you in?; **Saw yin an wan** (It is all the same).

Yince Same as **wance**.

Yiz You (plural, unemphatic).

Yoan That over there, often pronounced **thoan** or **roan**.

Youse You (plural, emphatic): **Thank youse, wan an aw!**

Yucky Bothered with an itch.

Yufty You are obliged to or ordered to: **Yufty go a message** (You are required to go on an errand).

Yurty Same as **yufty**.

Z

Zawfy It is terribly: **Zawfy caul** (It is terribly cold).

Zataw Is that the finish?

Zataw? Ay, adzaw!